MOTLEY MANDALAS 3:

50 MORE DETAILED DESIGNS

FOR ADULTS TO COLOR

BY

JACQUELINE WISNIEWSKI

Thank you for purchasing MOTLEY MANDALAS 3: 50 MORE DETAILED DESIGNS FOR ADULTS TO COLOR.

For best results I suggest tearing out the page you want to color and coloring it separately from the rest of the book. If you bend the spine backwards in multiple spots it should open more flatly, making it easier to tear out each page cleanly.

Please note:
- All images are one-sided for the best coloring experience.
- The mandalas with background images are meant to be cut down to approximately 8 x 8, which is why the background images do not fill the entire page.
- Unfortunately the publisher only offers one kind of paper weight, so I strongly suggest not using alcohol-based markers in this coloring book, as they will bleed through significantly. However other types of markers, gel pens, and colored pencils will work wonderfully.

Grab your favorite supplies, get comfortable, and enjoy the relaxing experience of coloring Motley Mandalas! When finished, please share your work of art online at:
www.Facebook.com/MotleyMandalas/

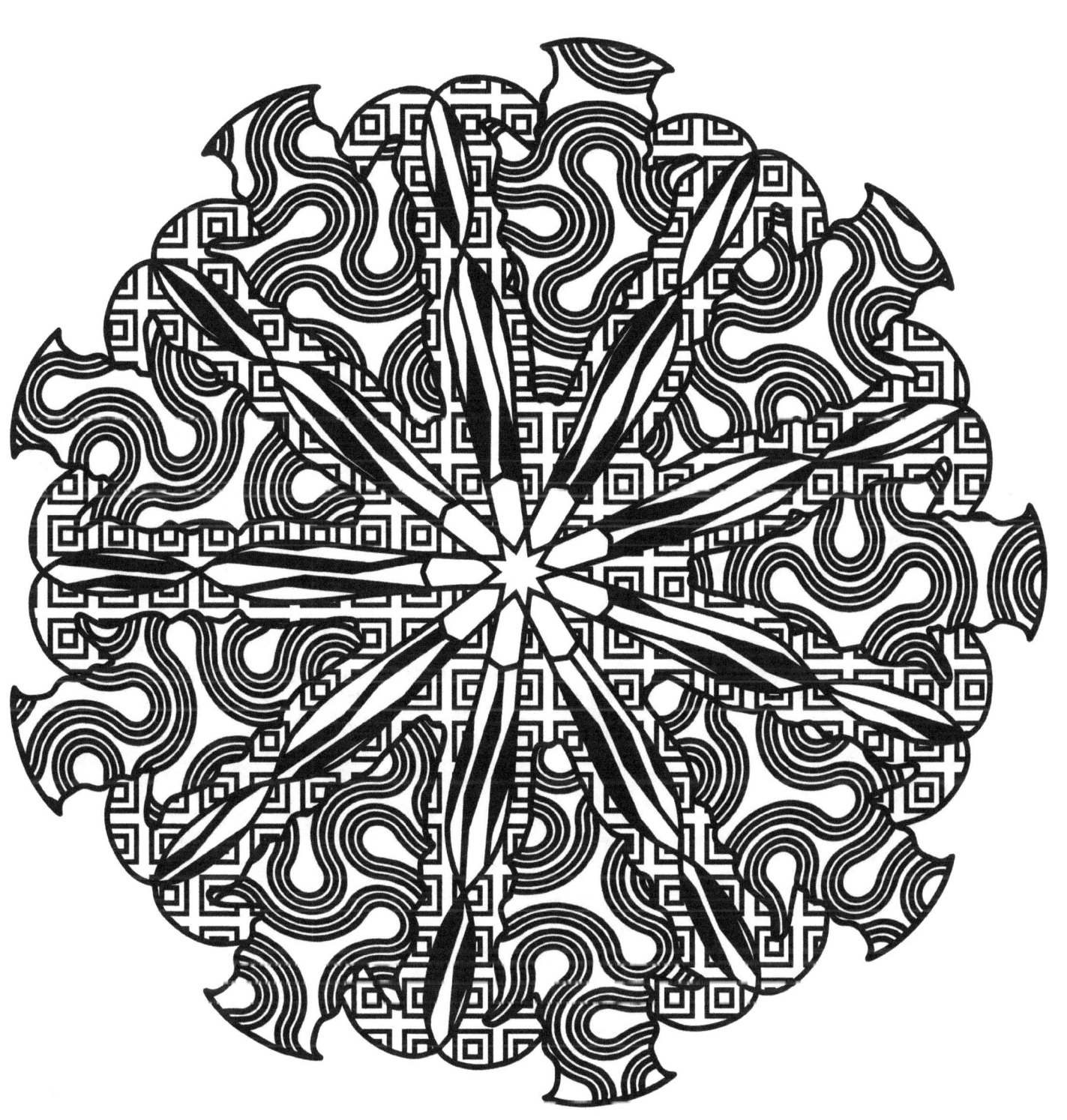

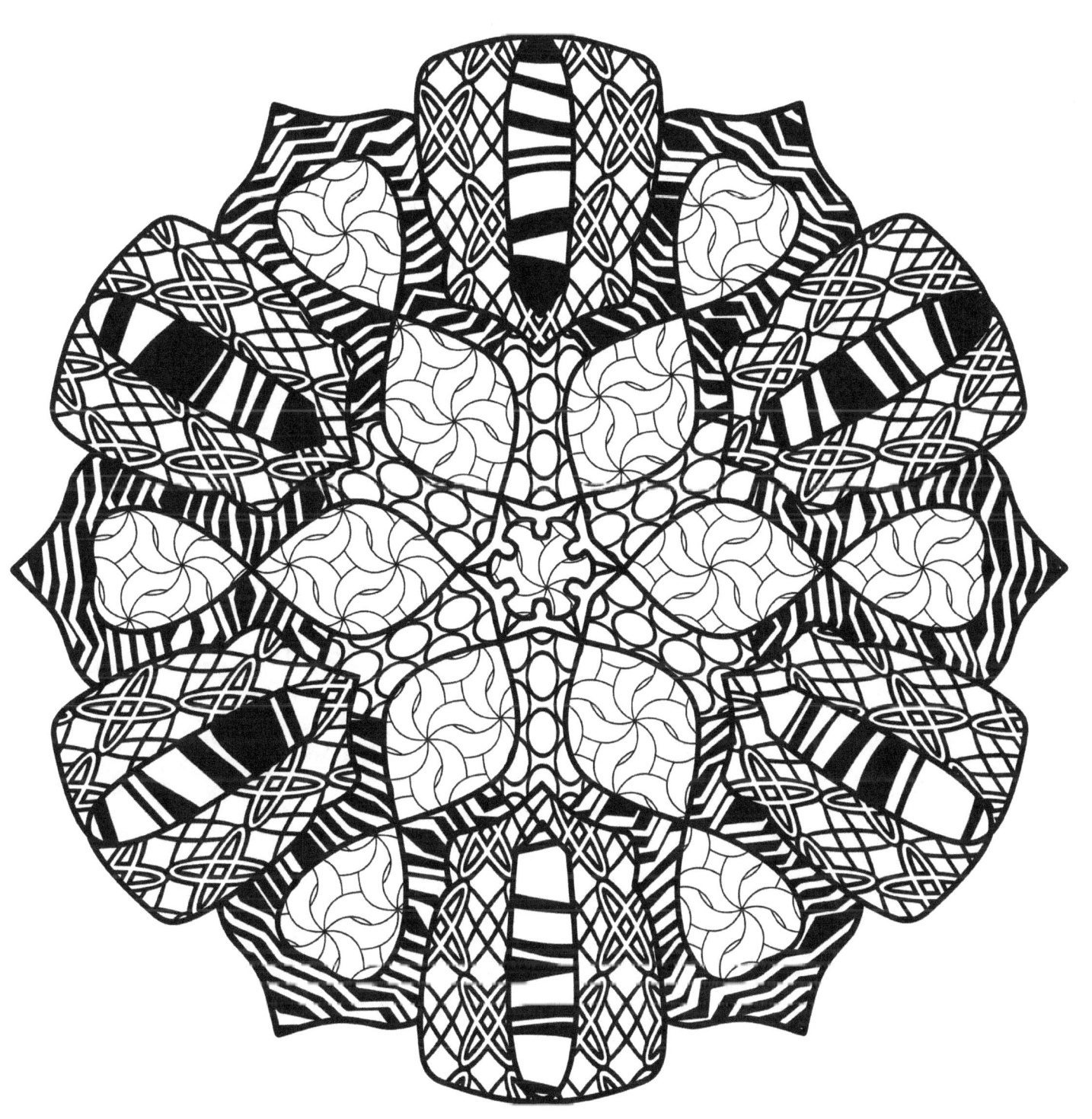

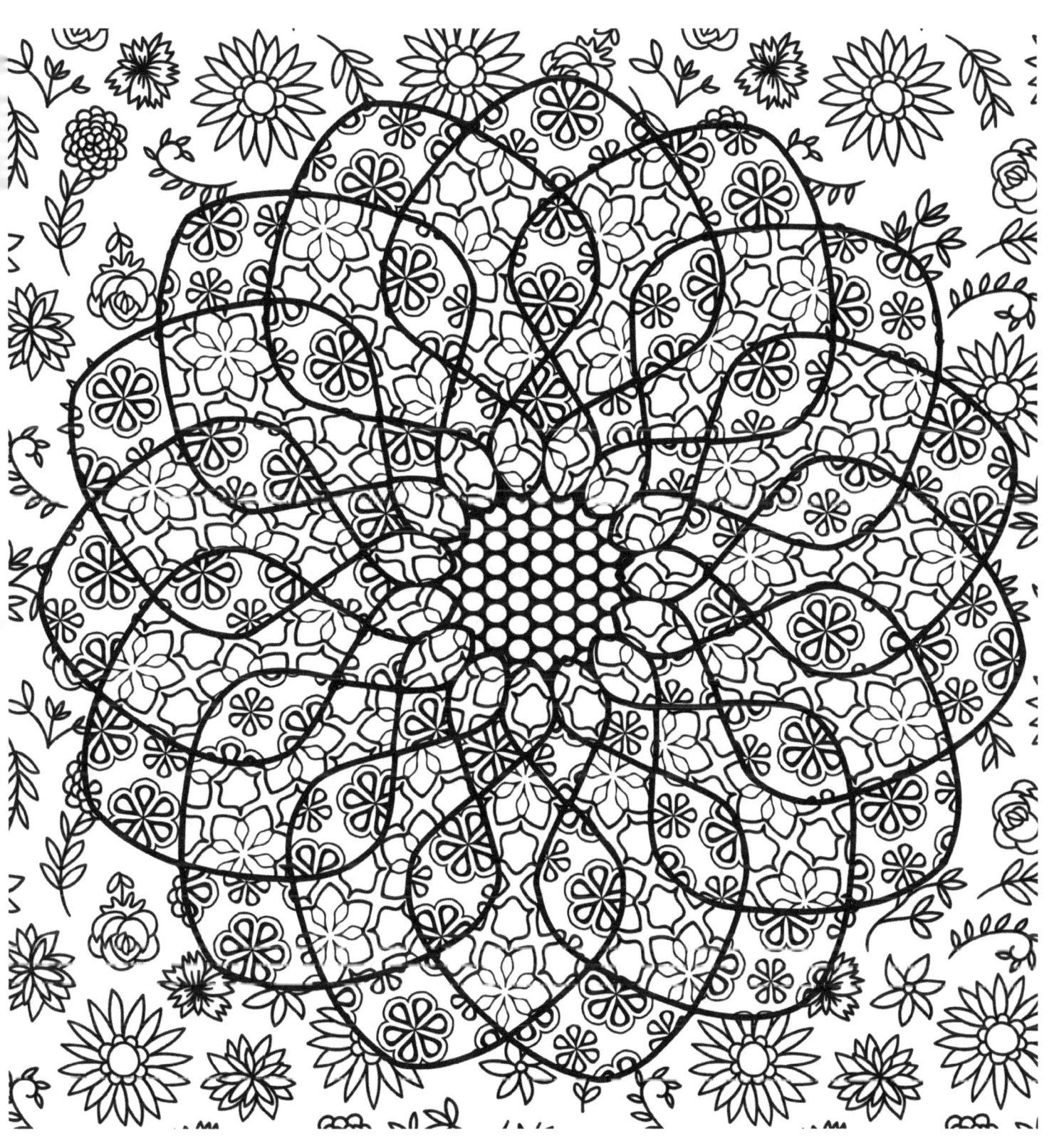

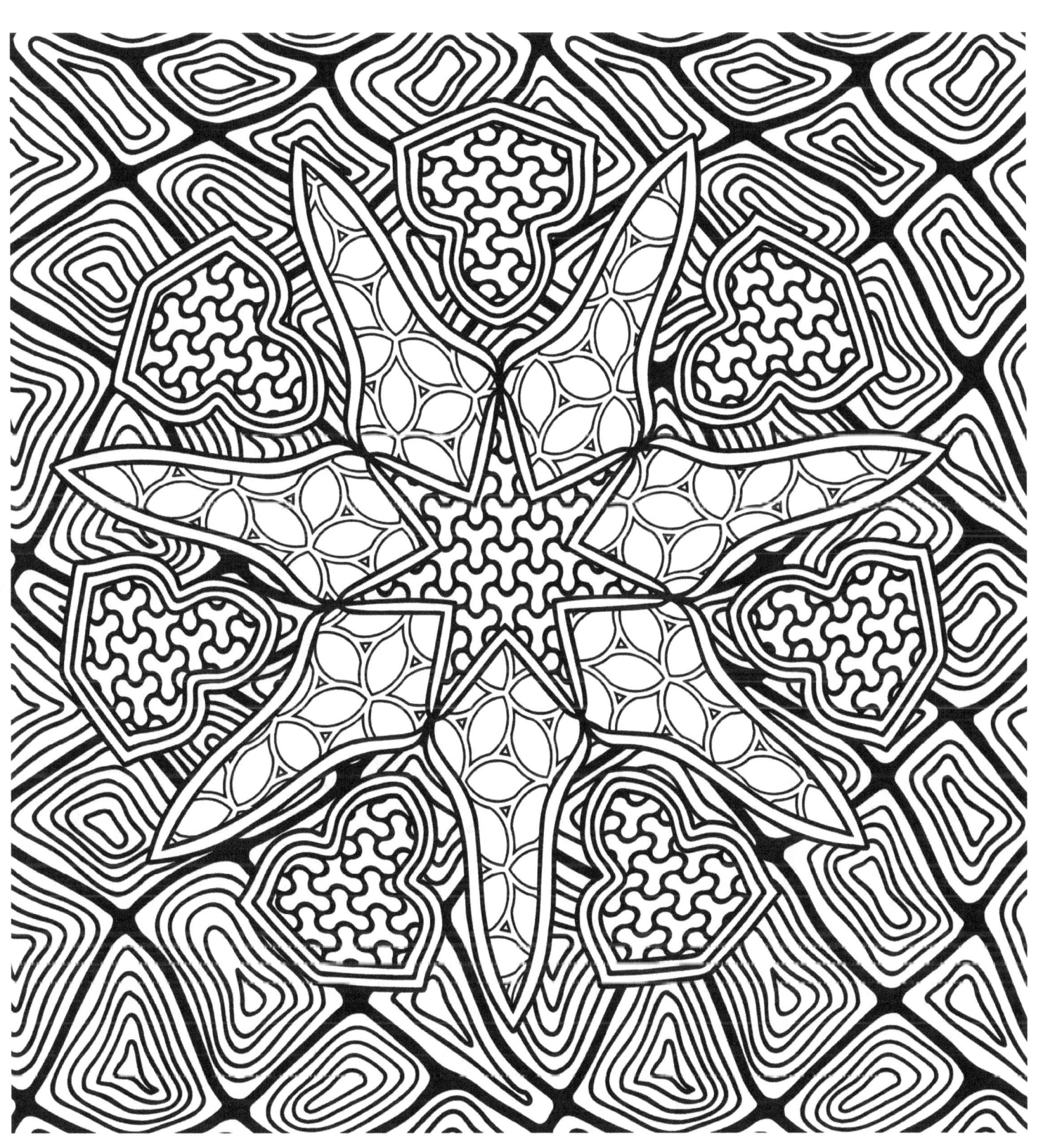

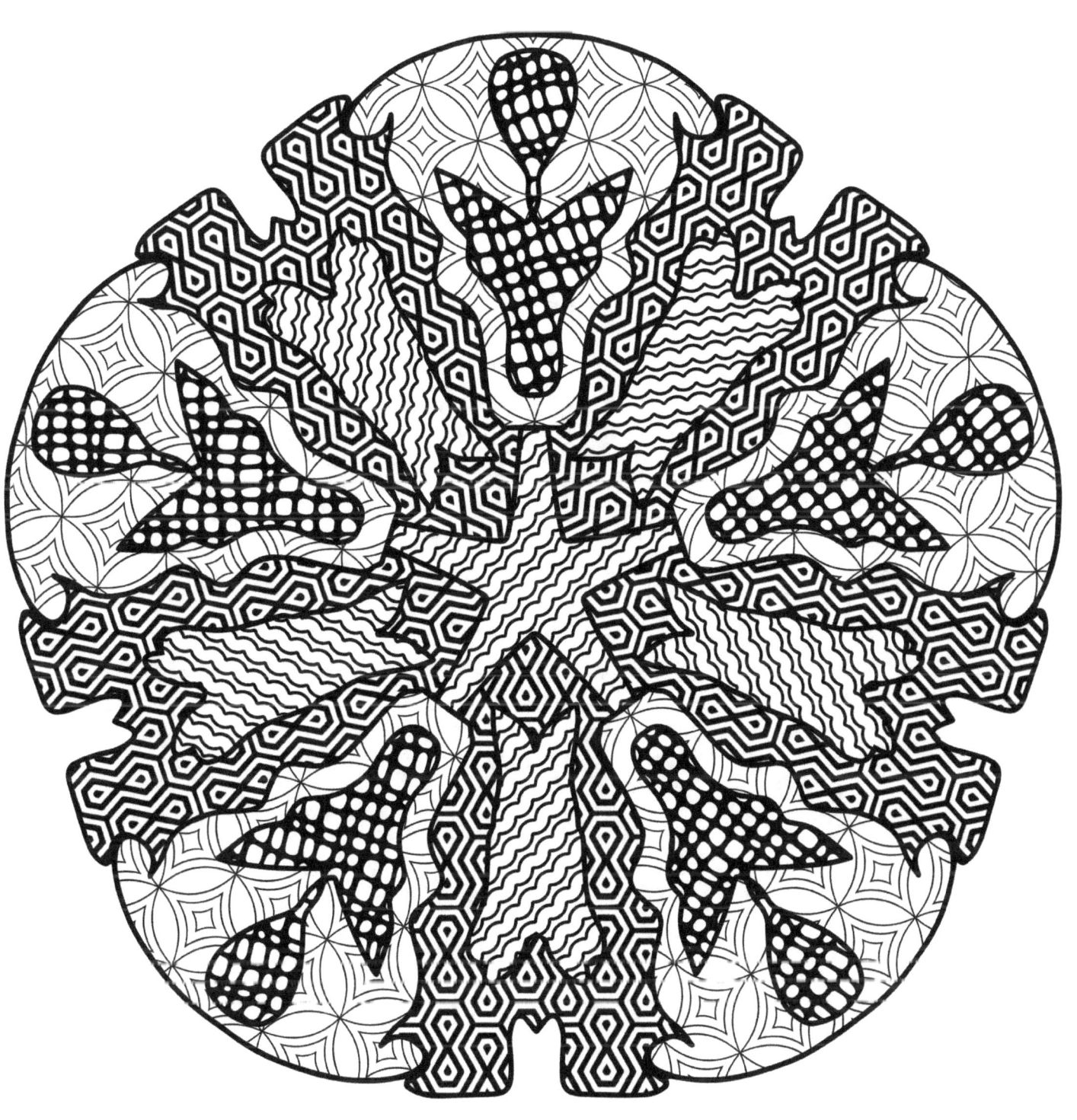

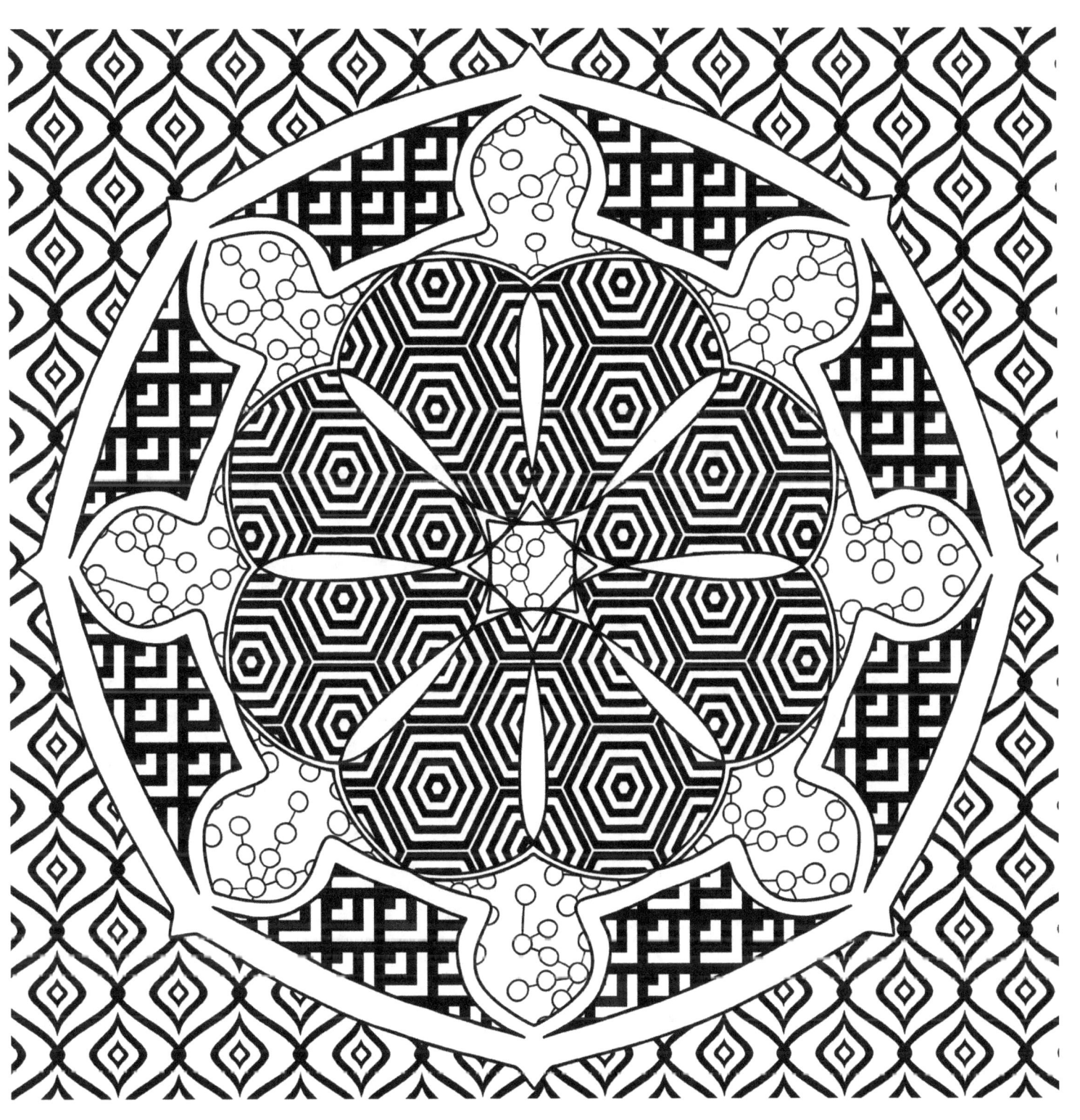

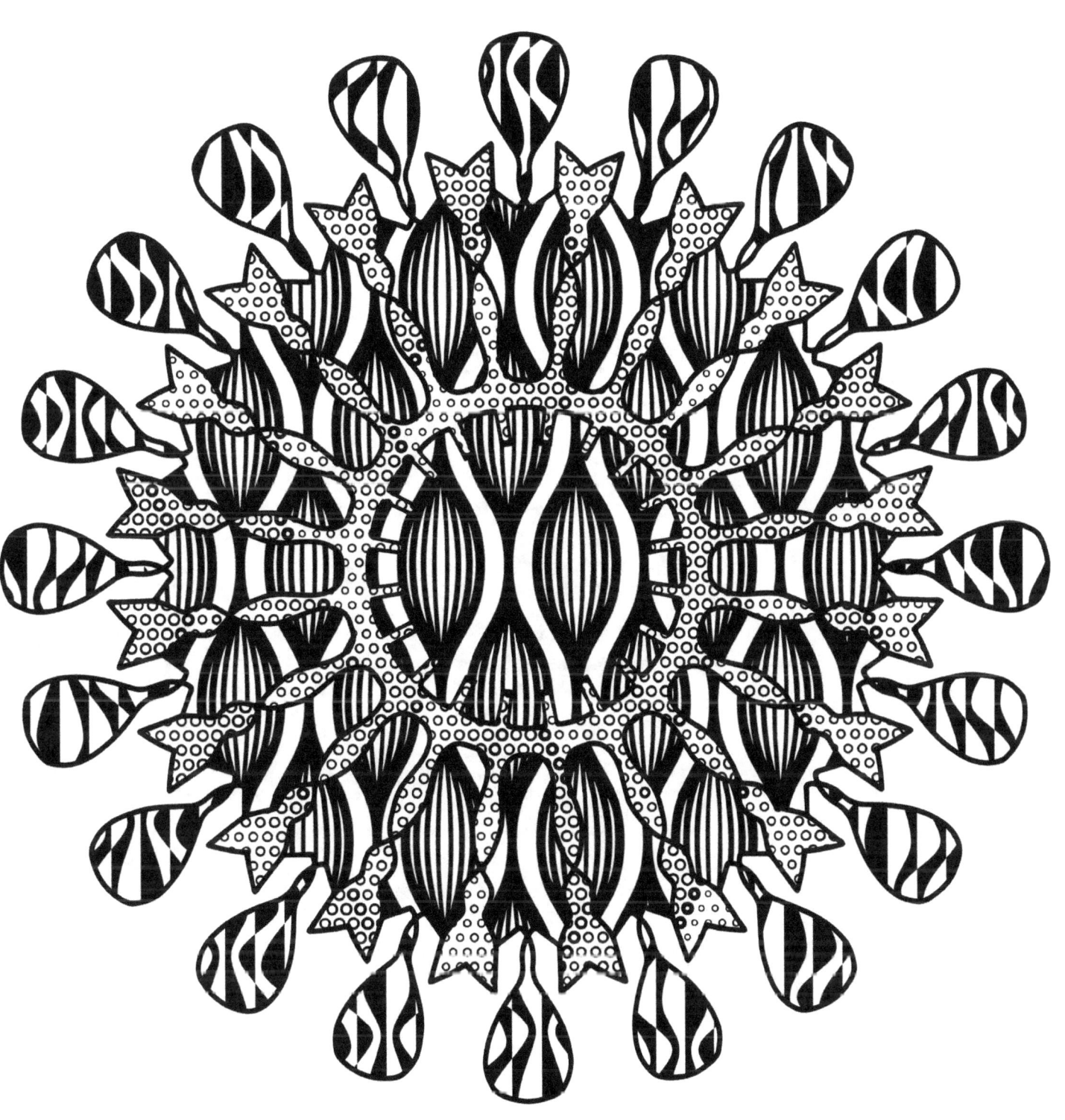

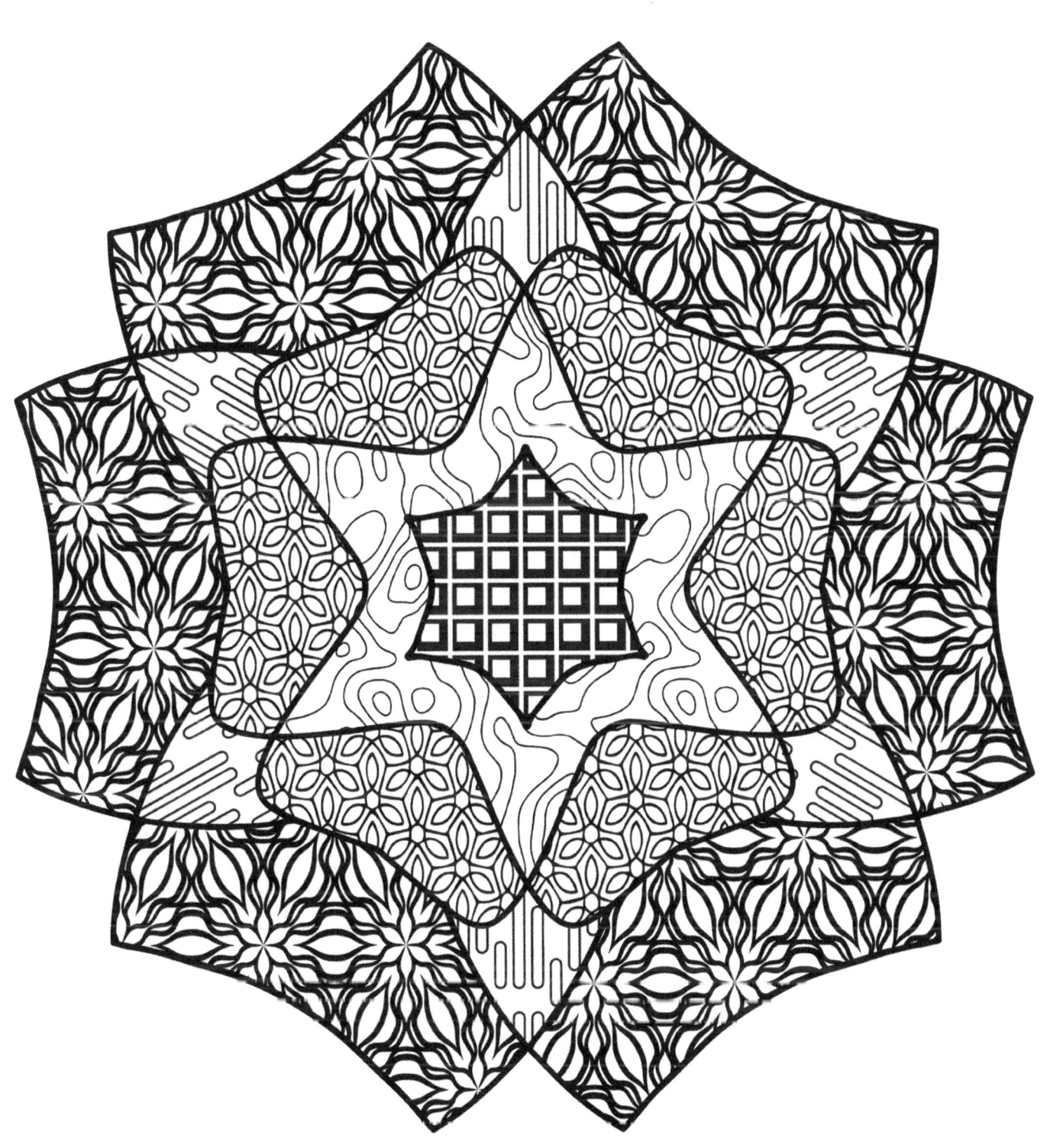

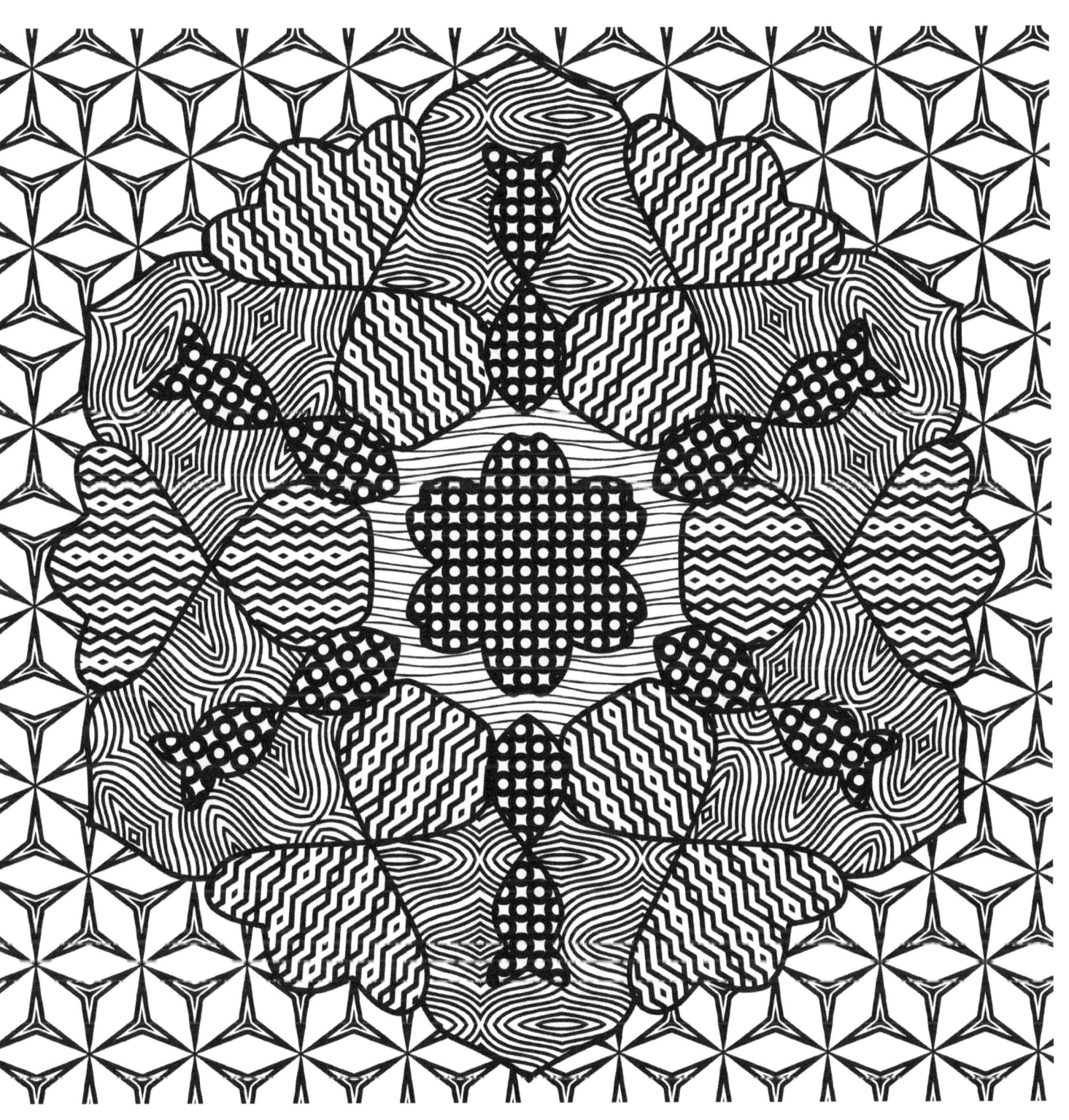

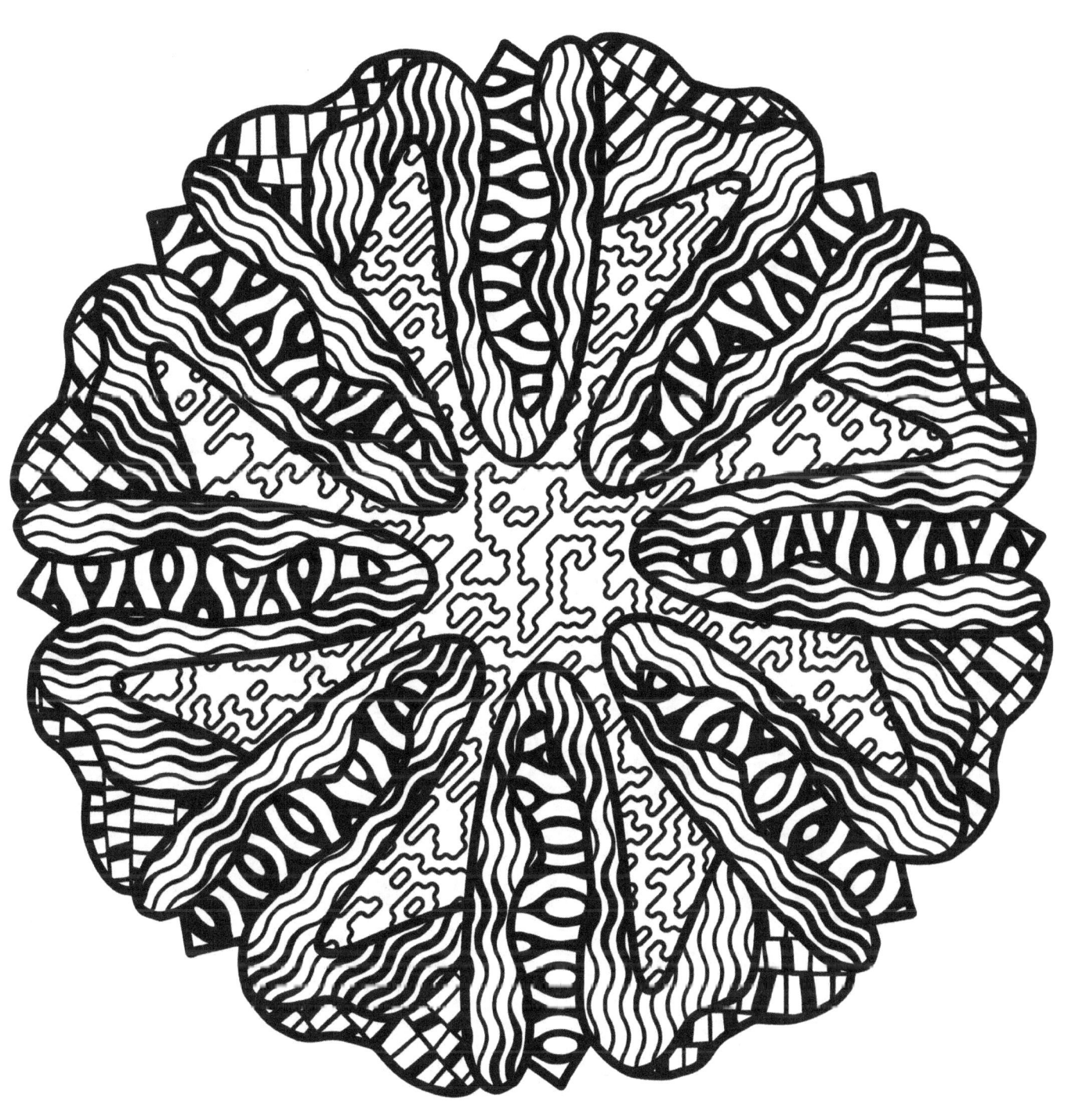

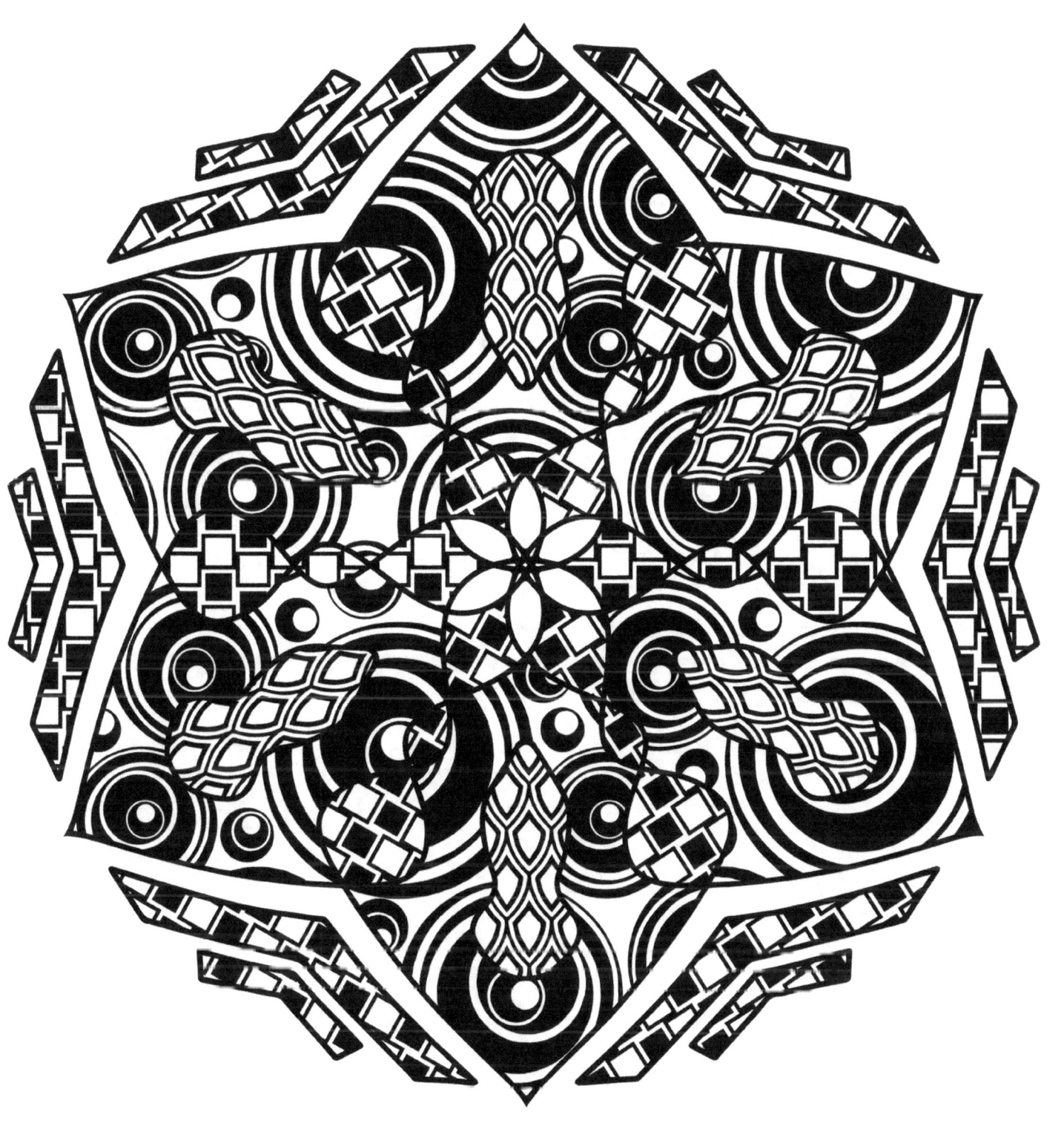

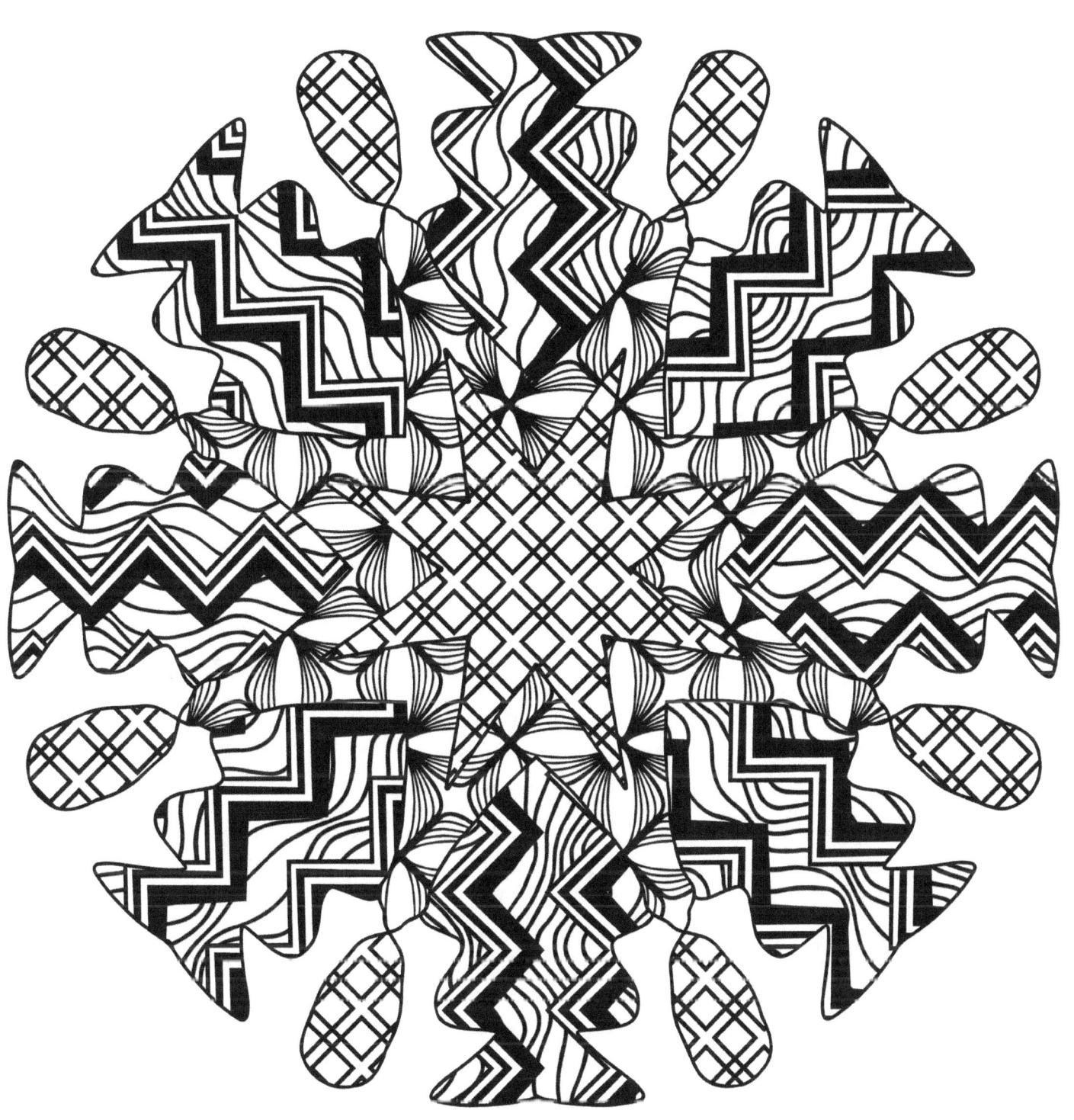

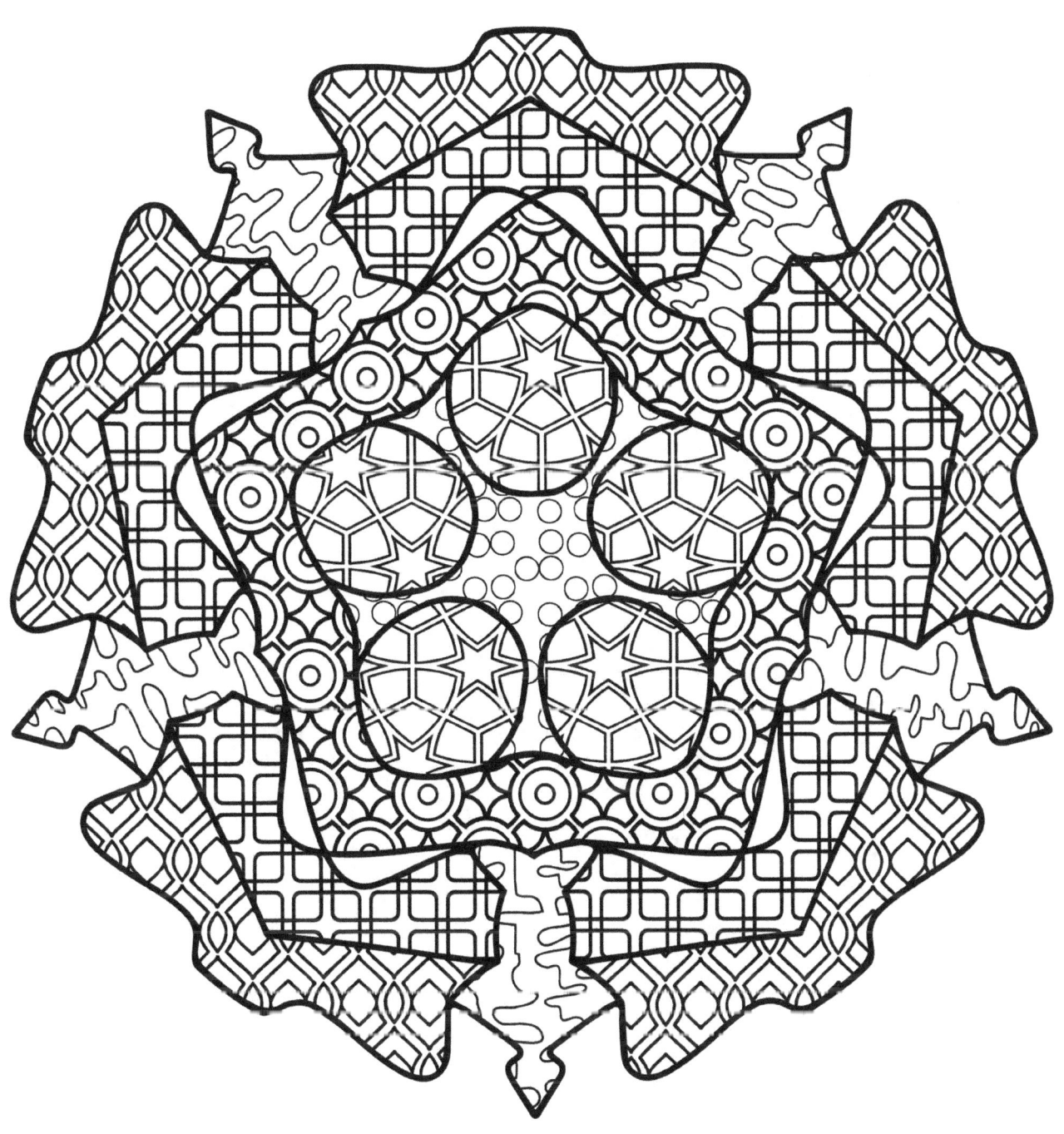

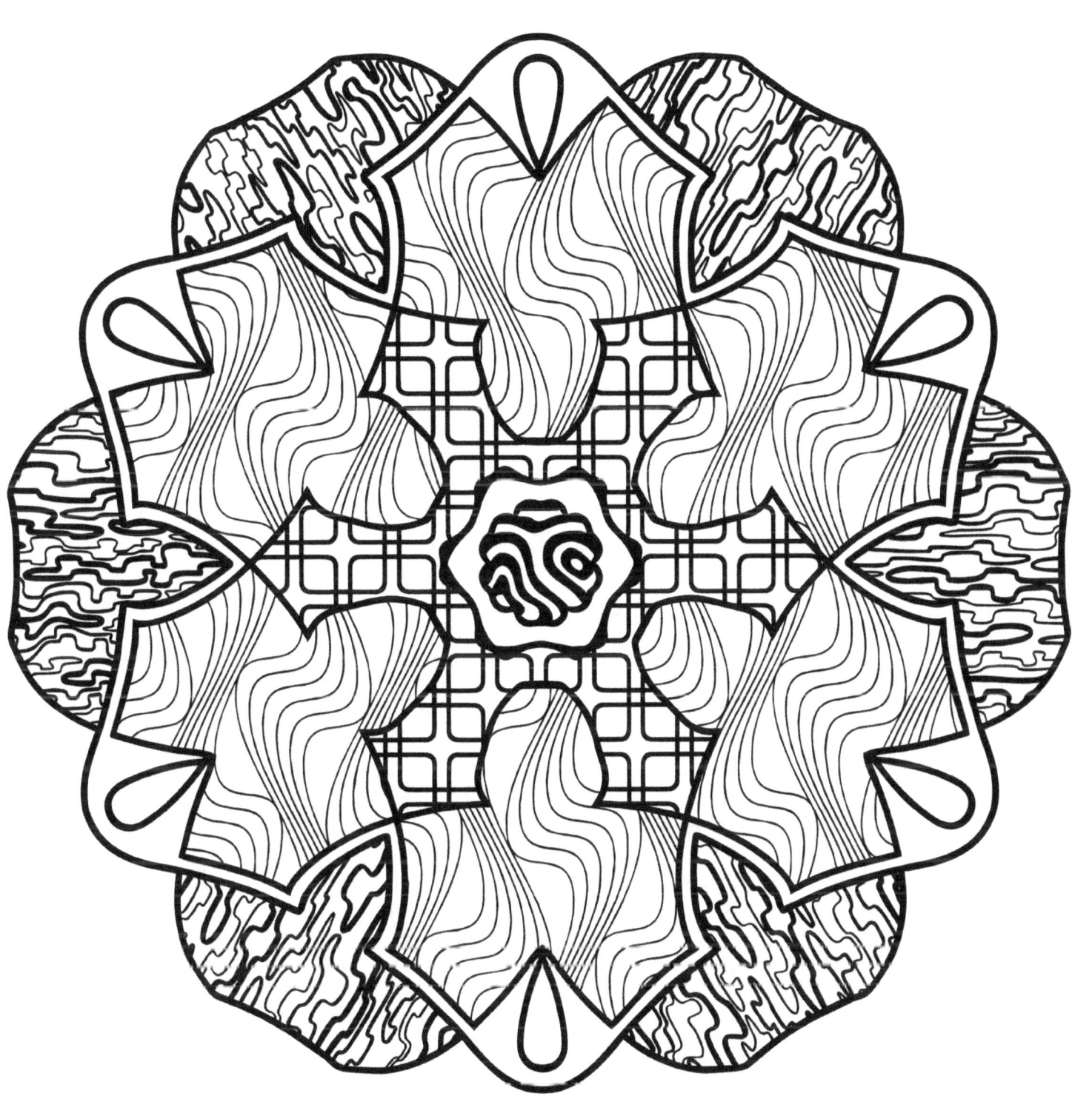

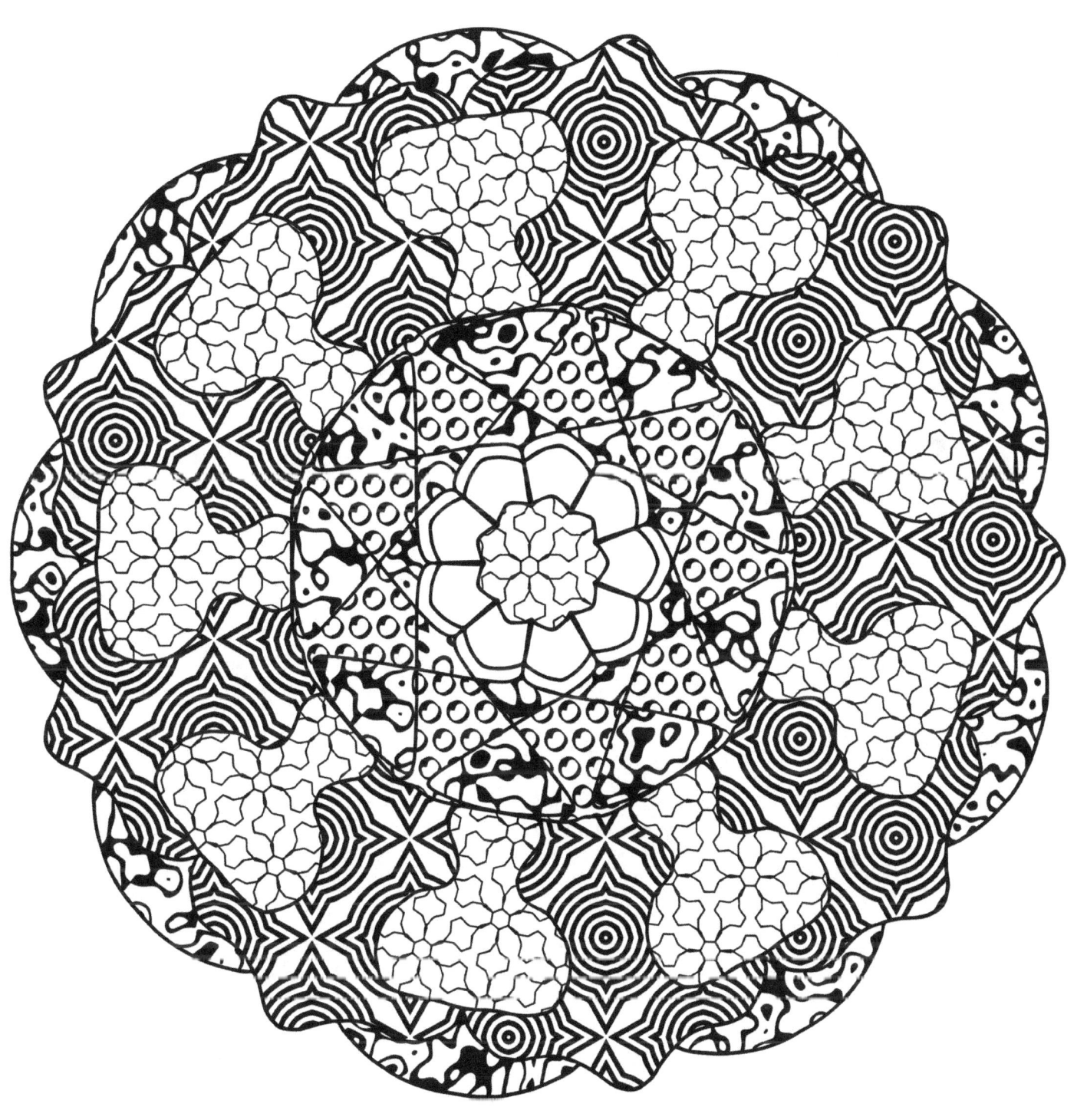

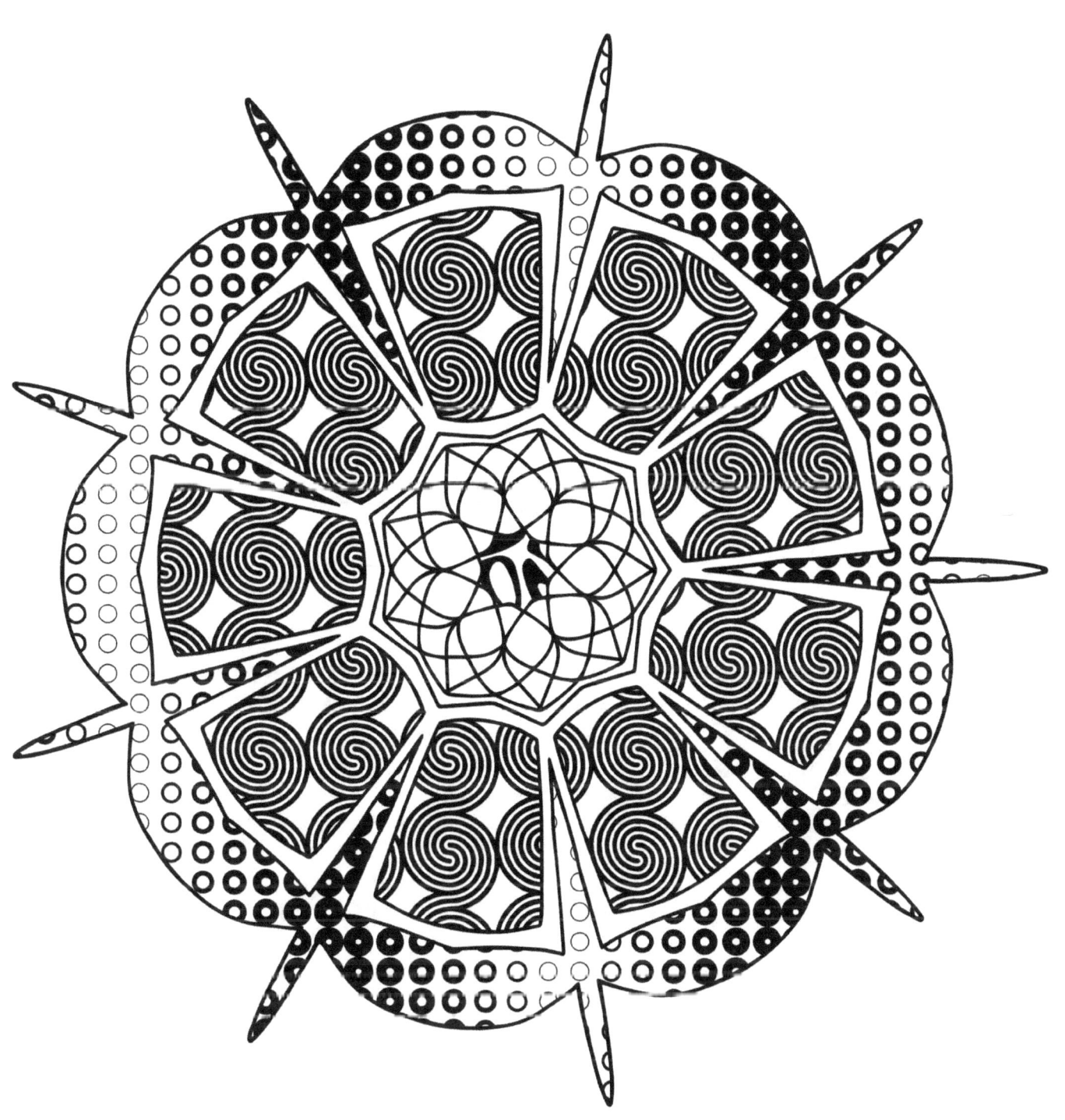

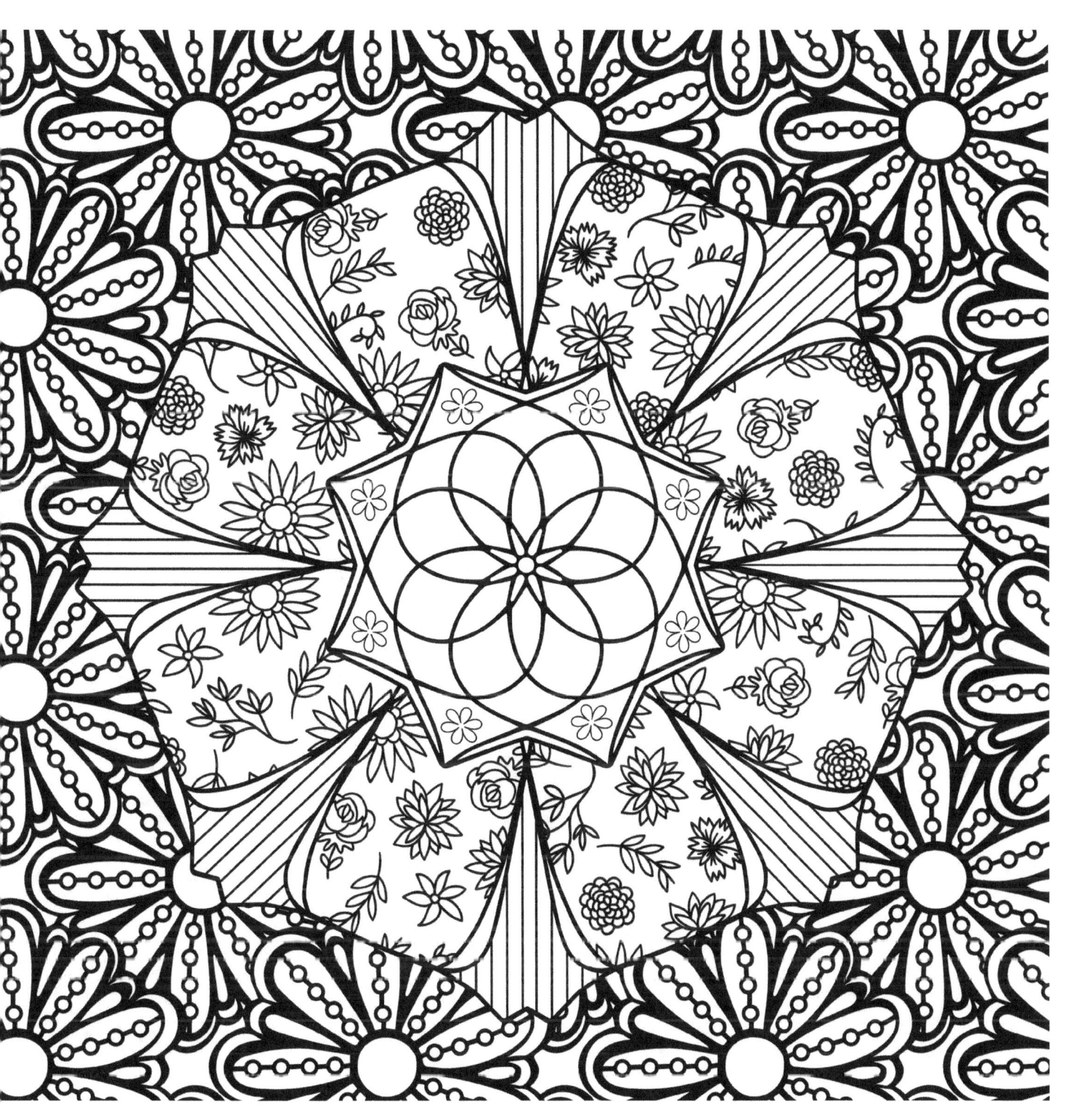

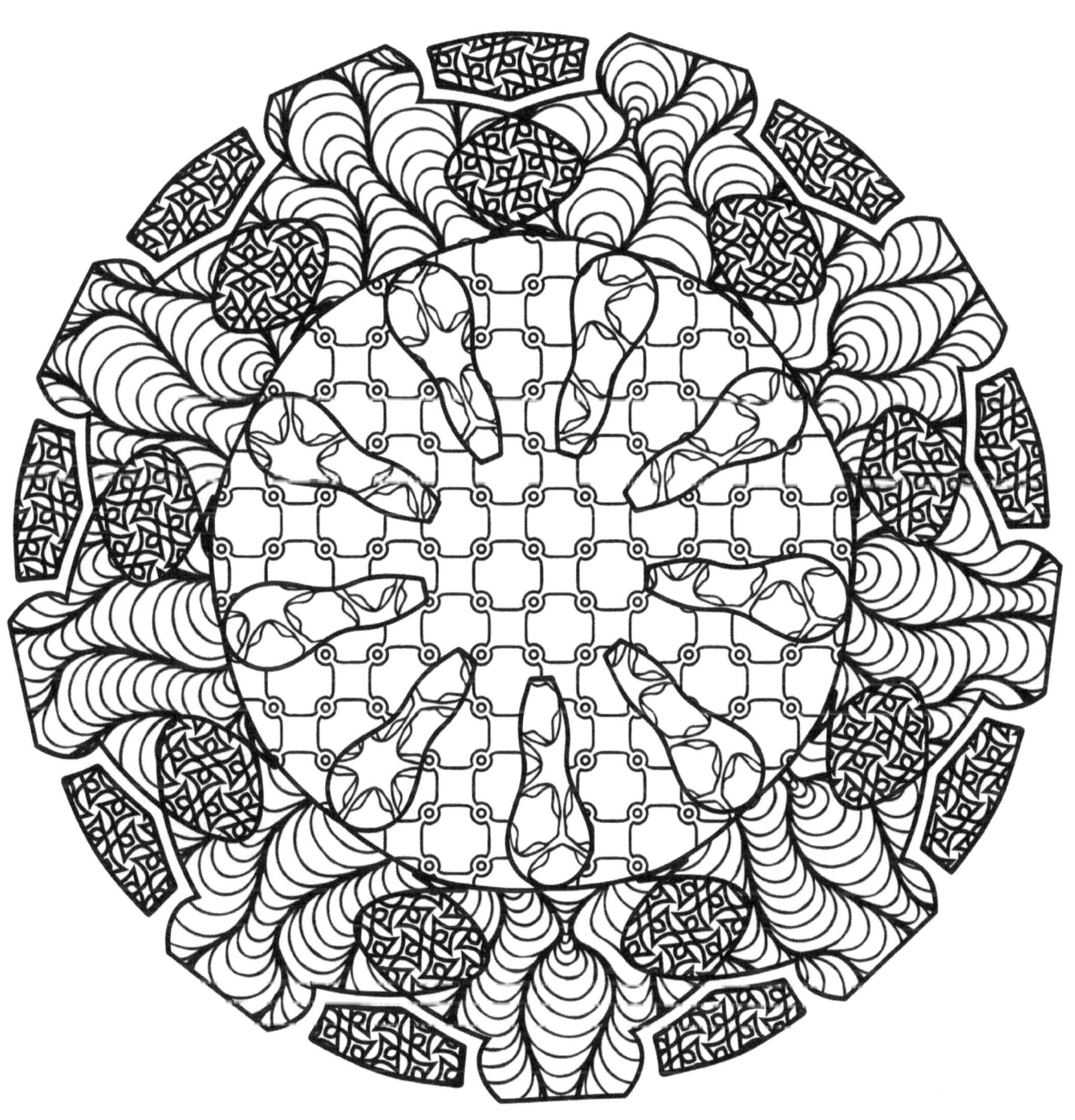

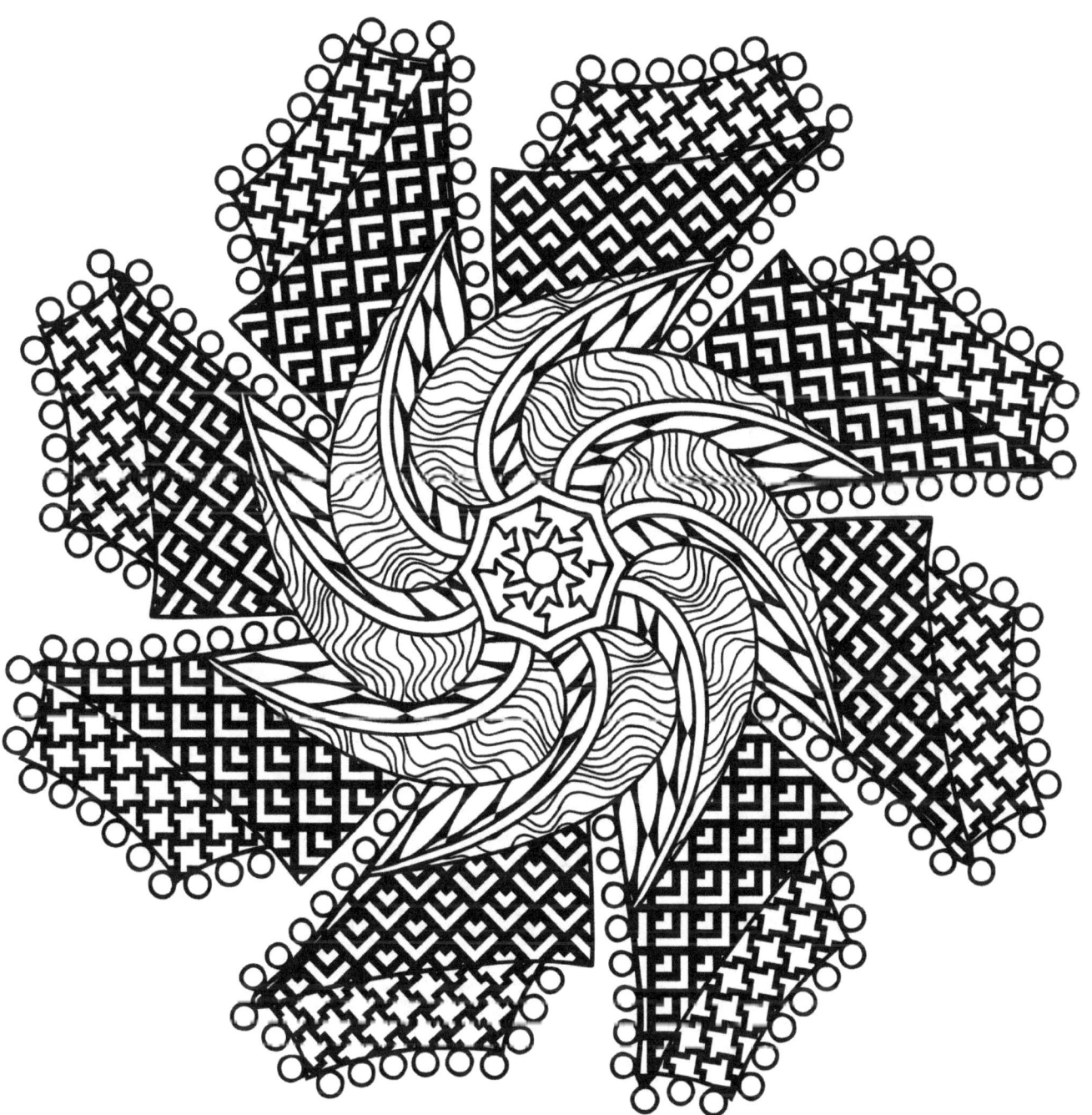

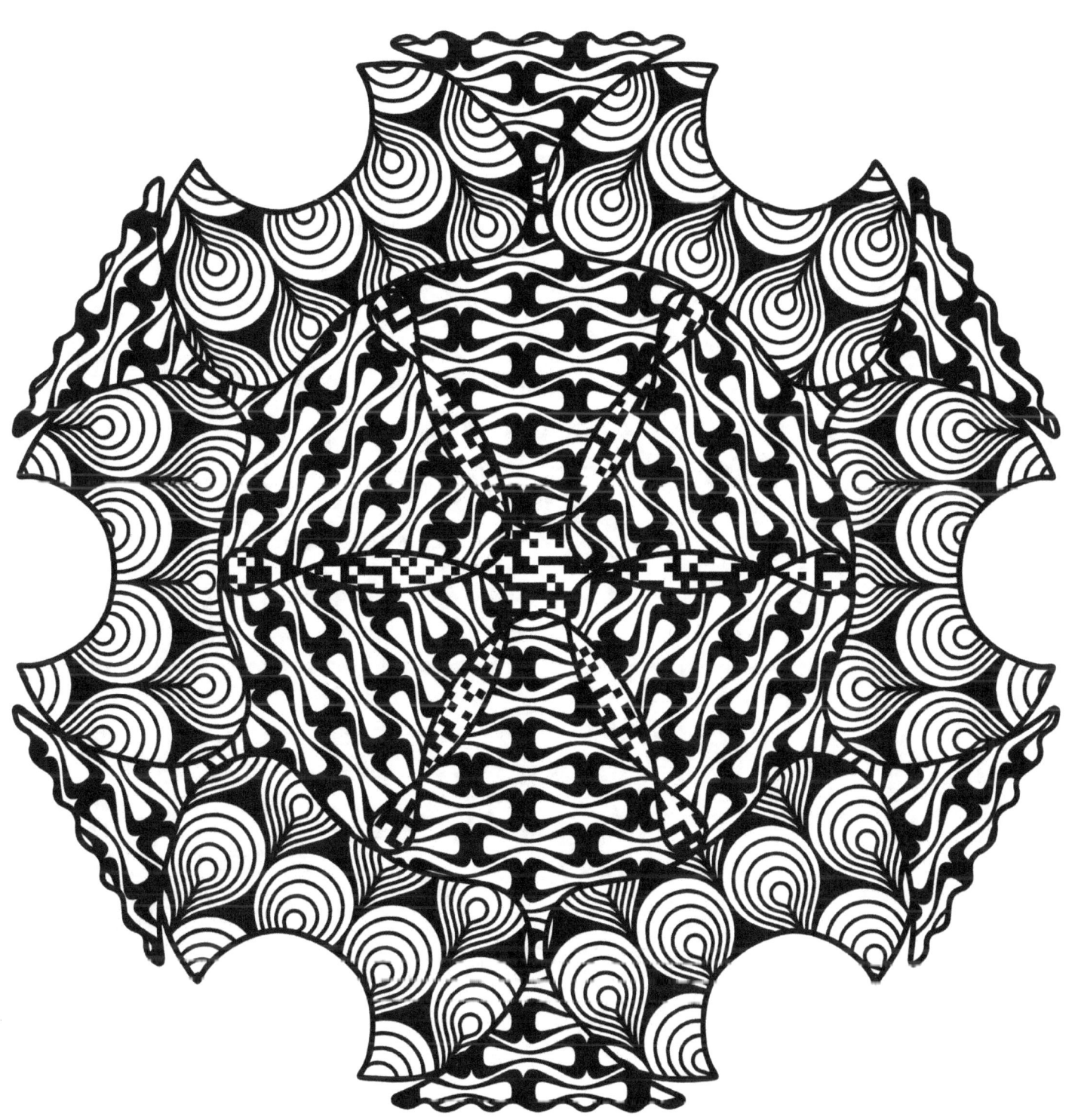

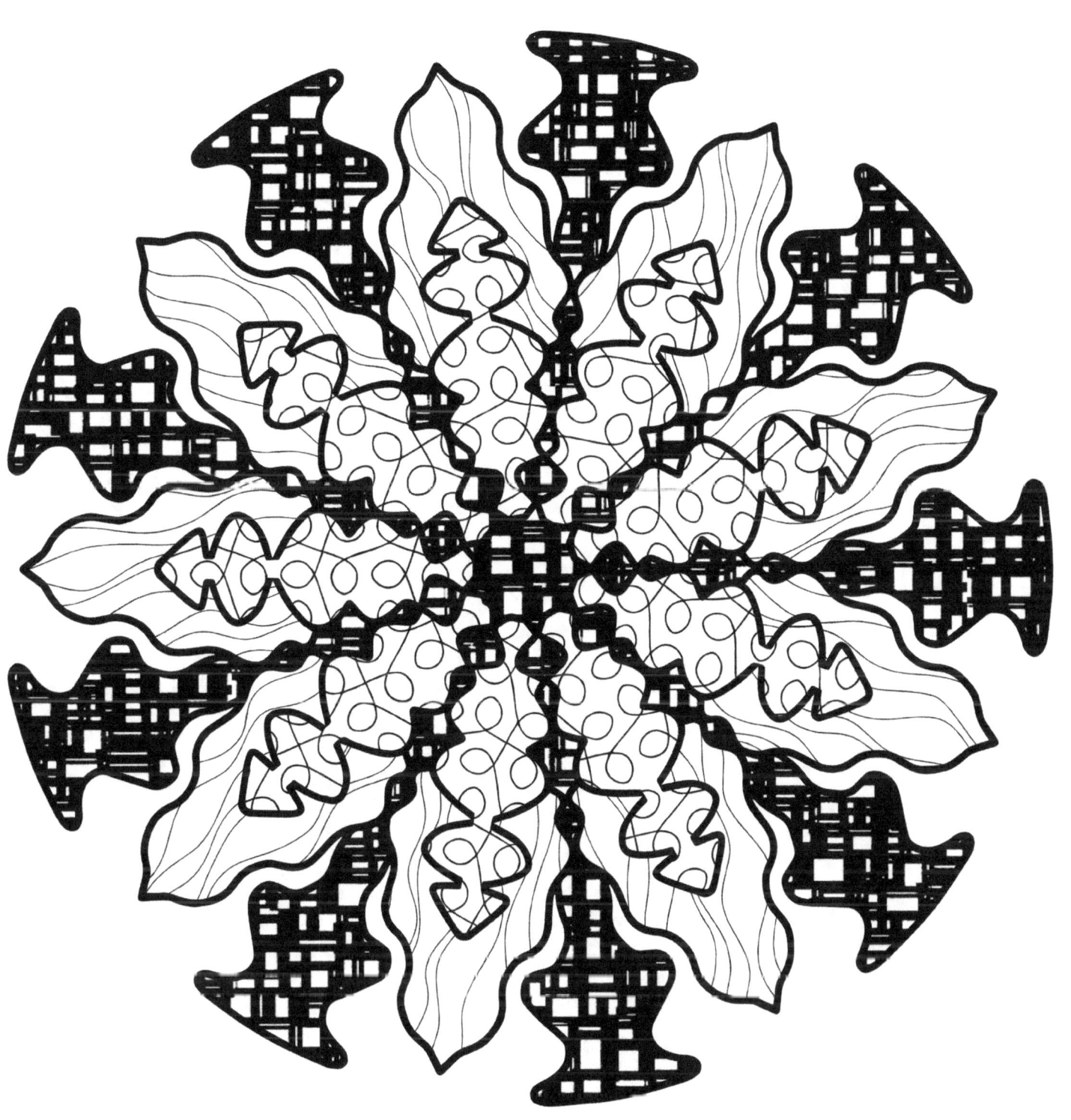

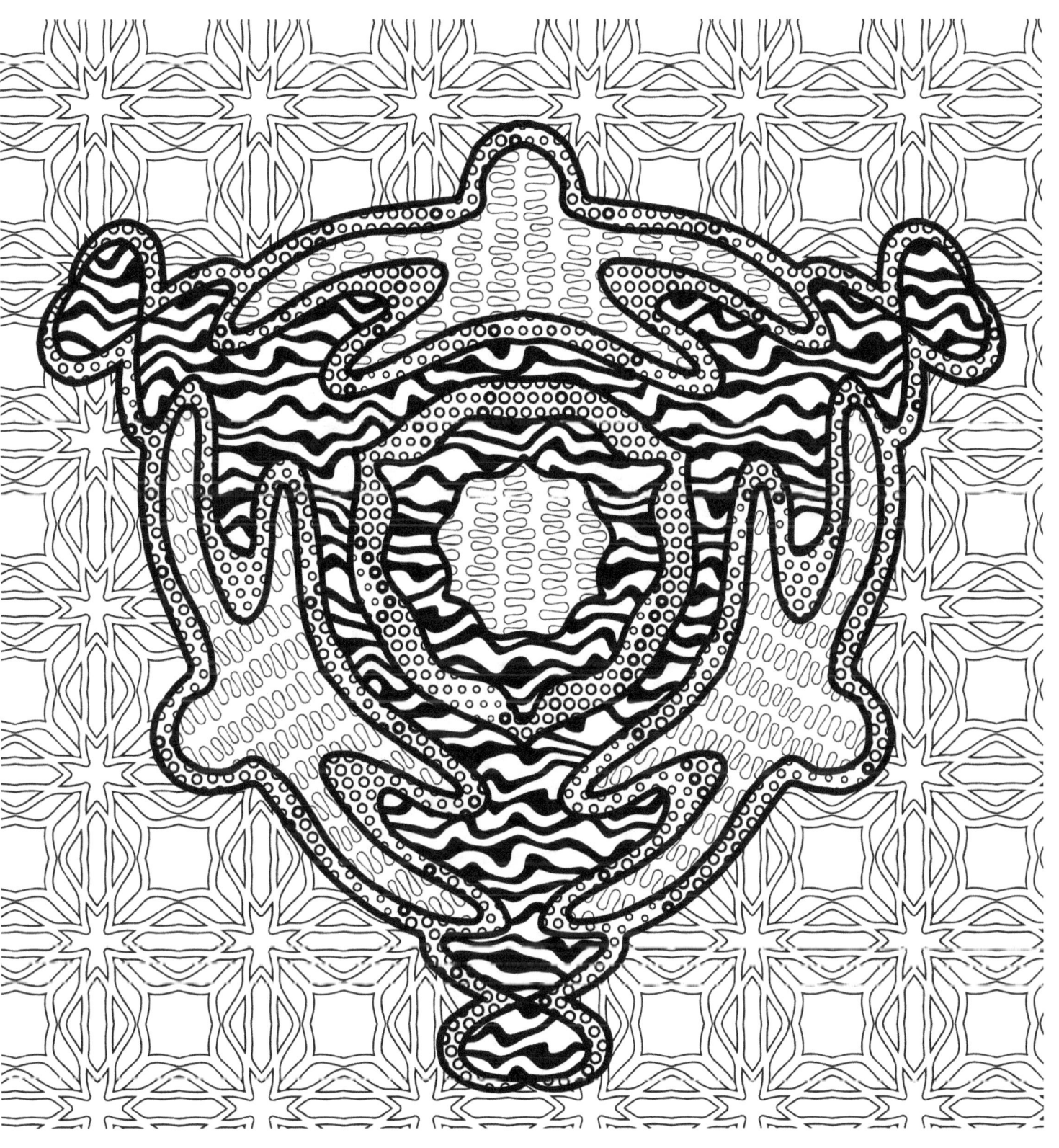

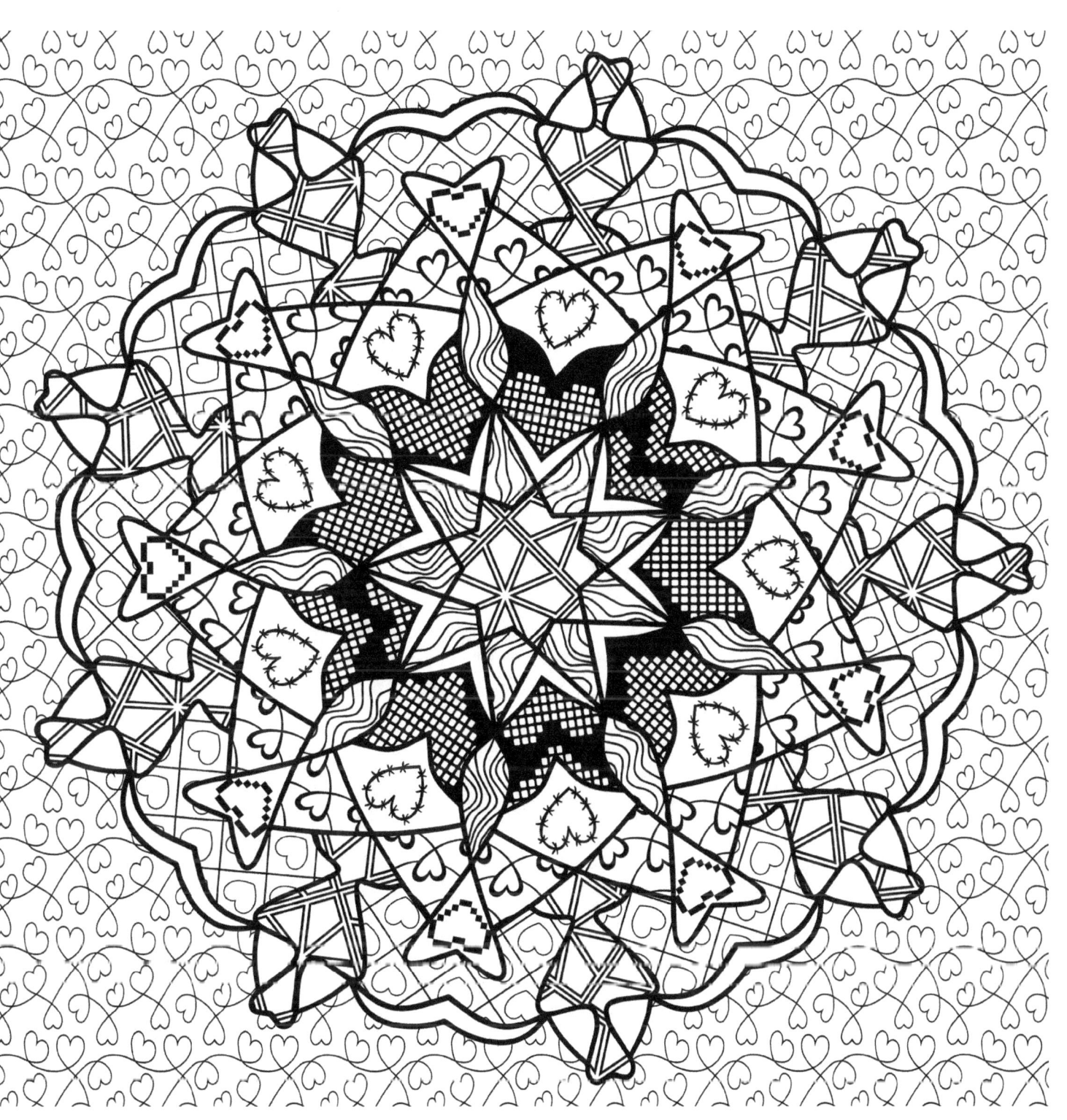

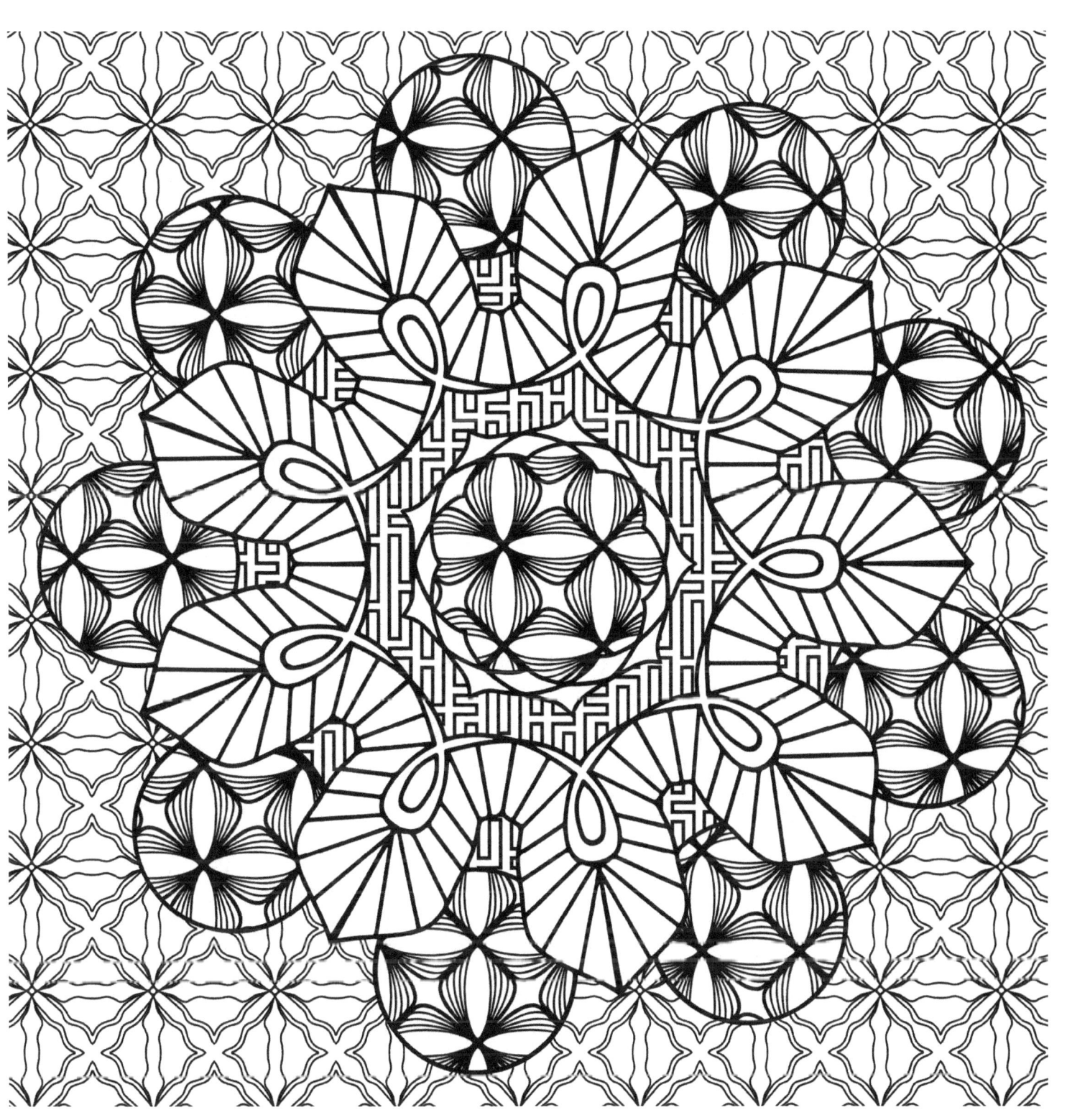

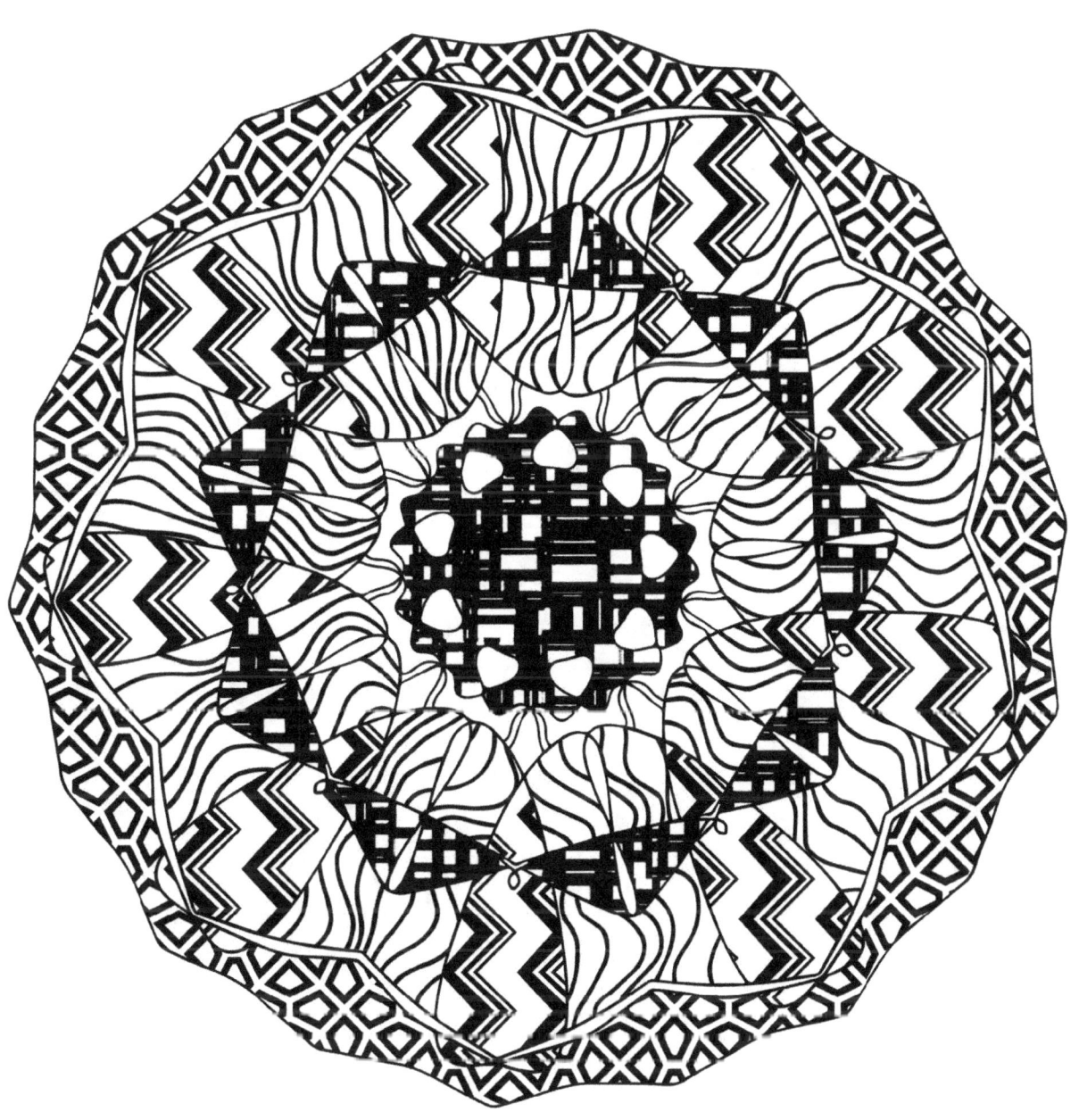

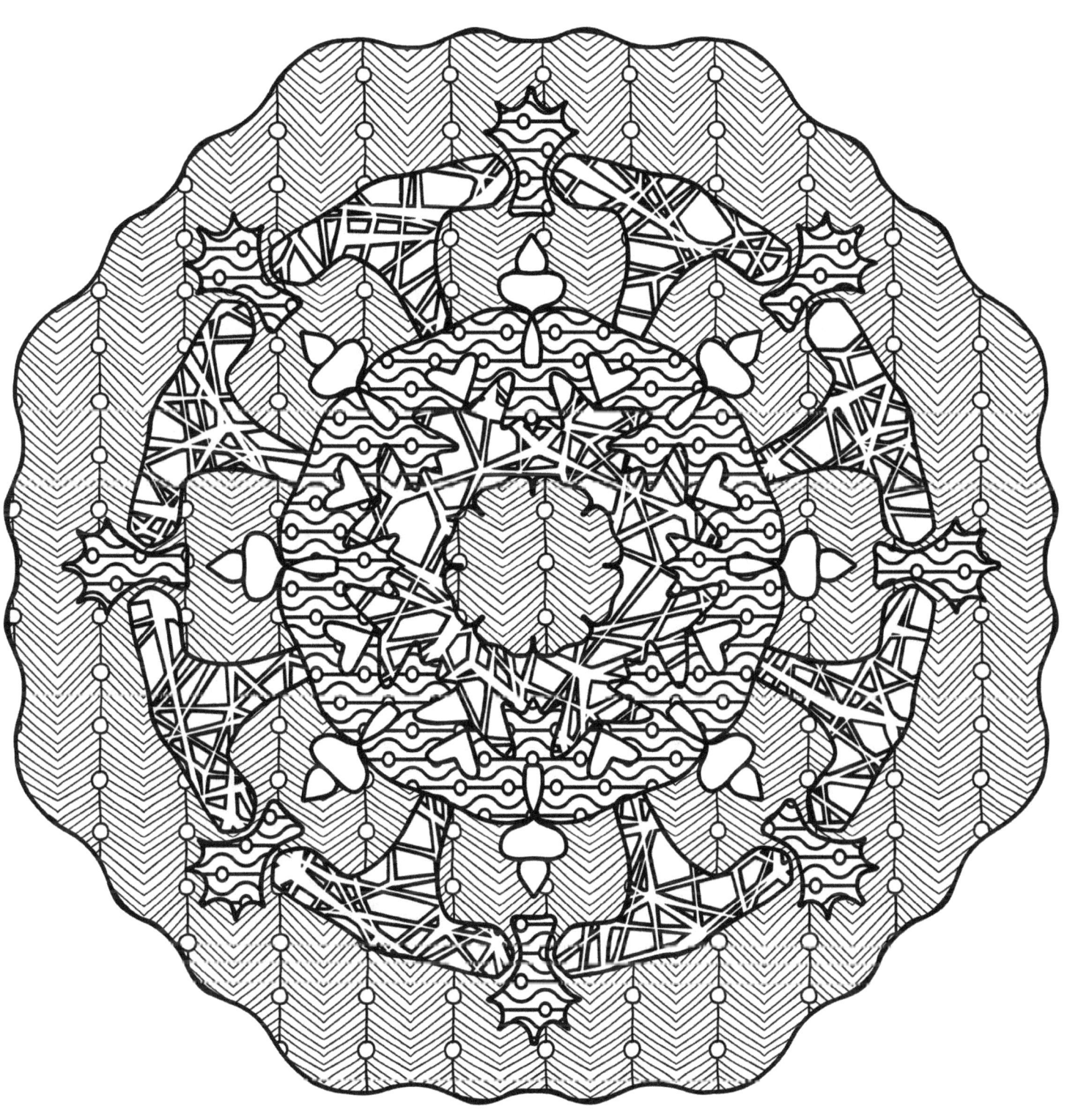

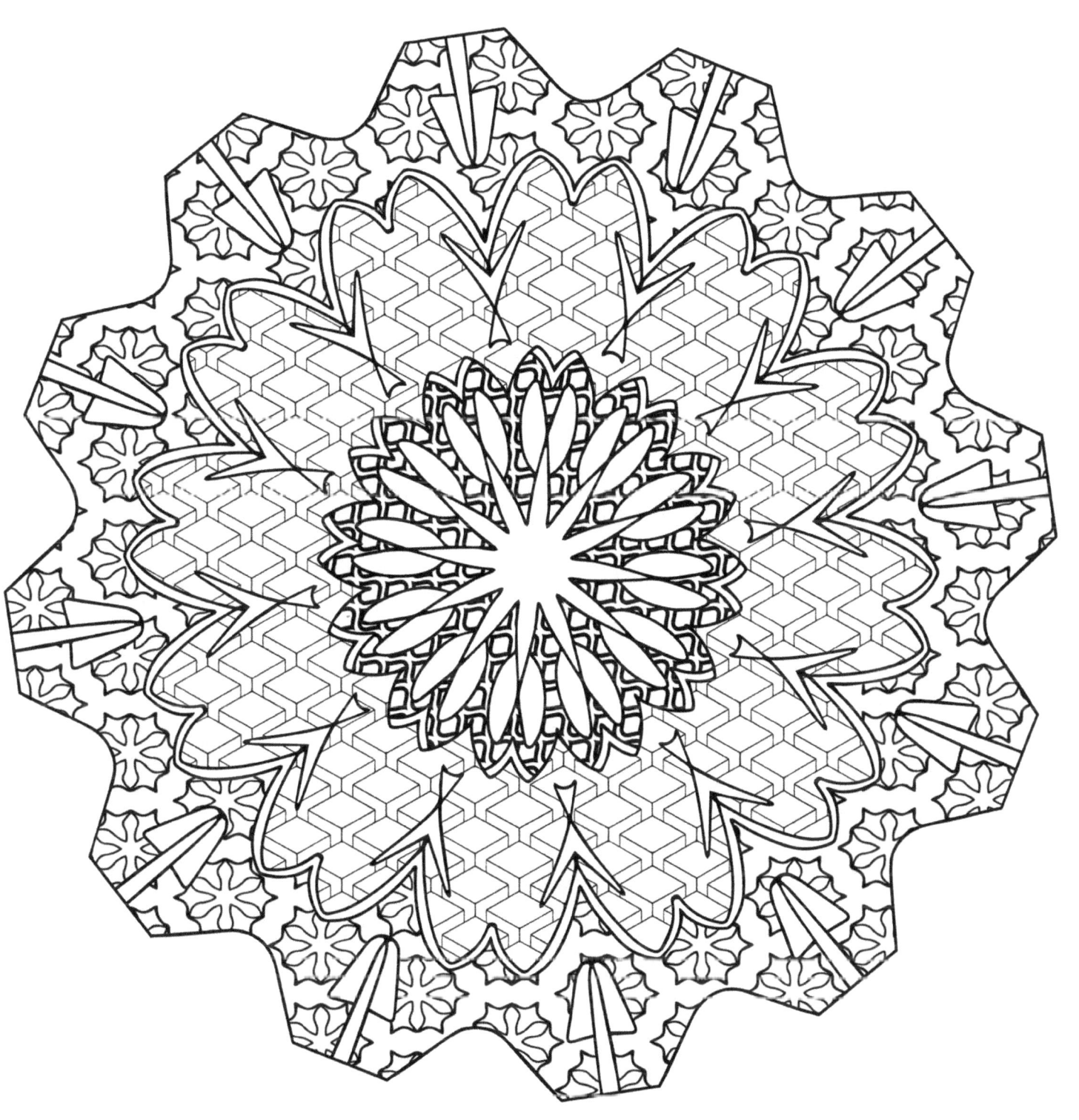

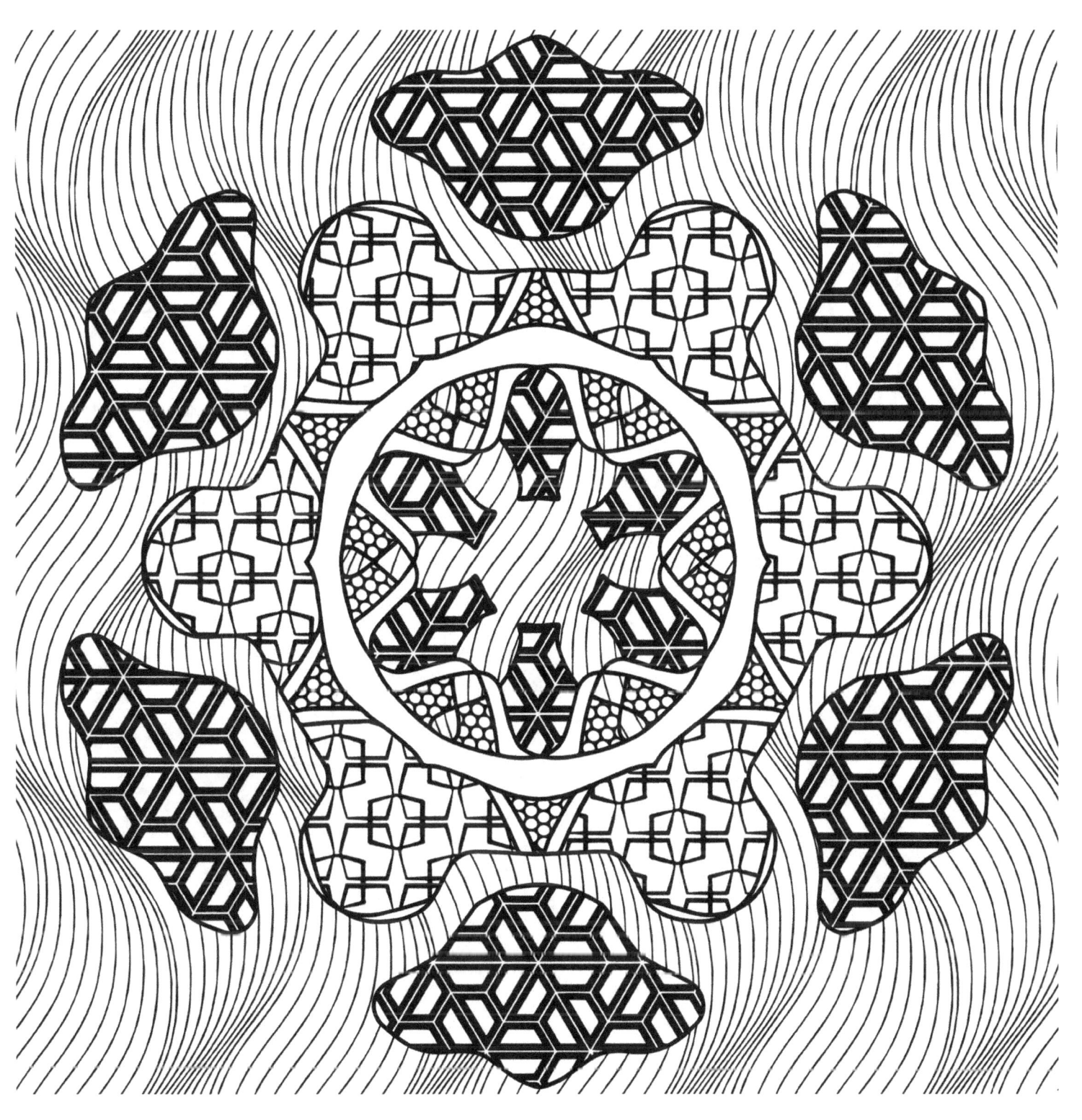

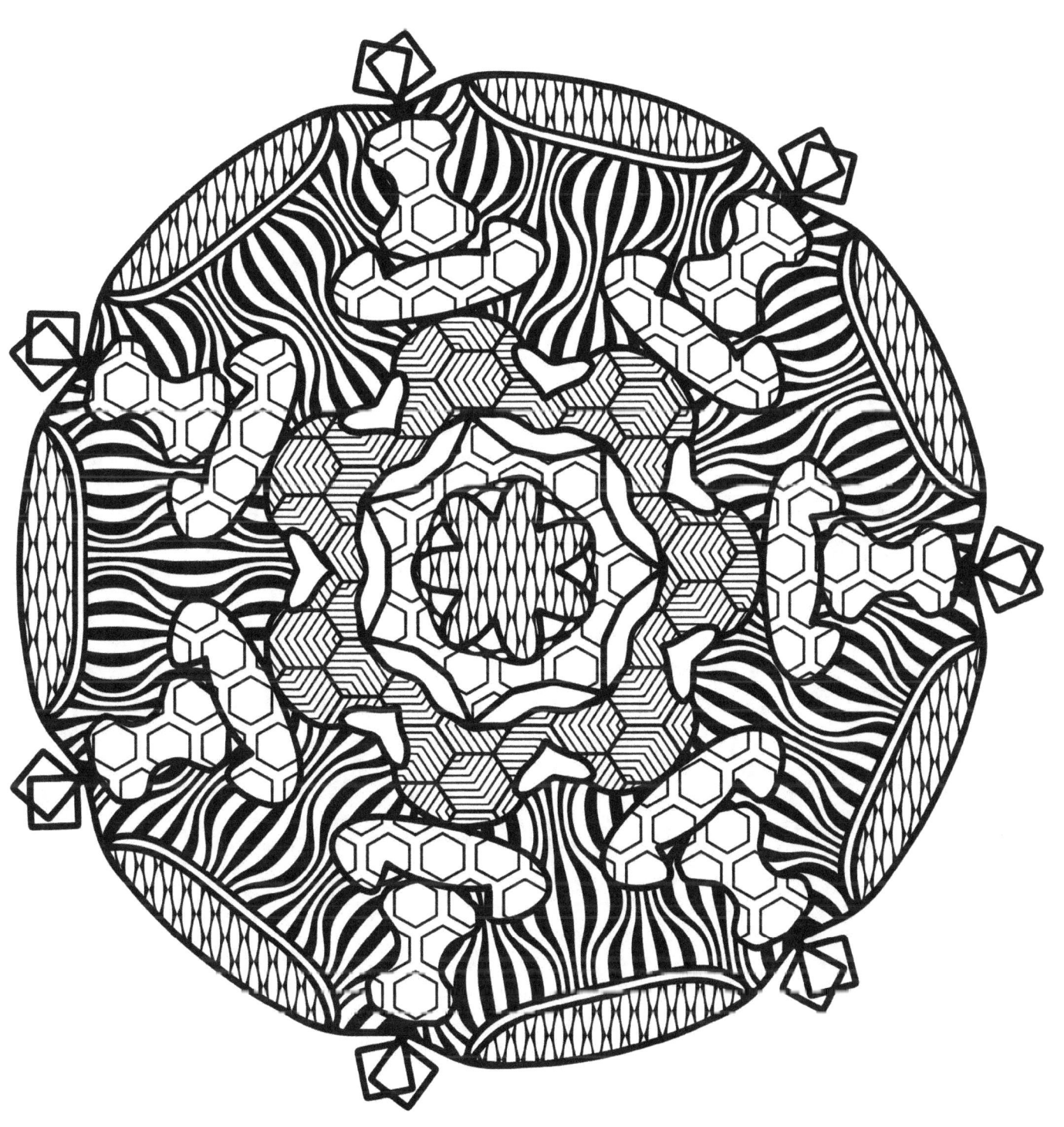

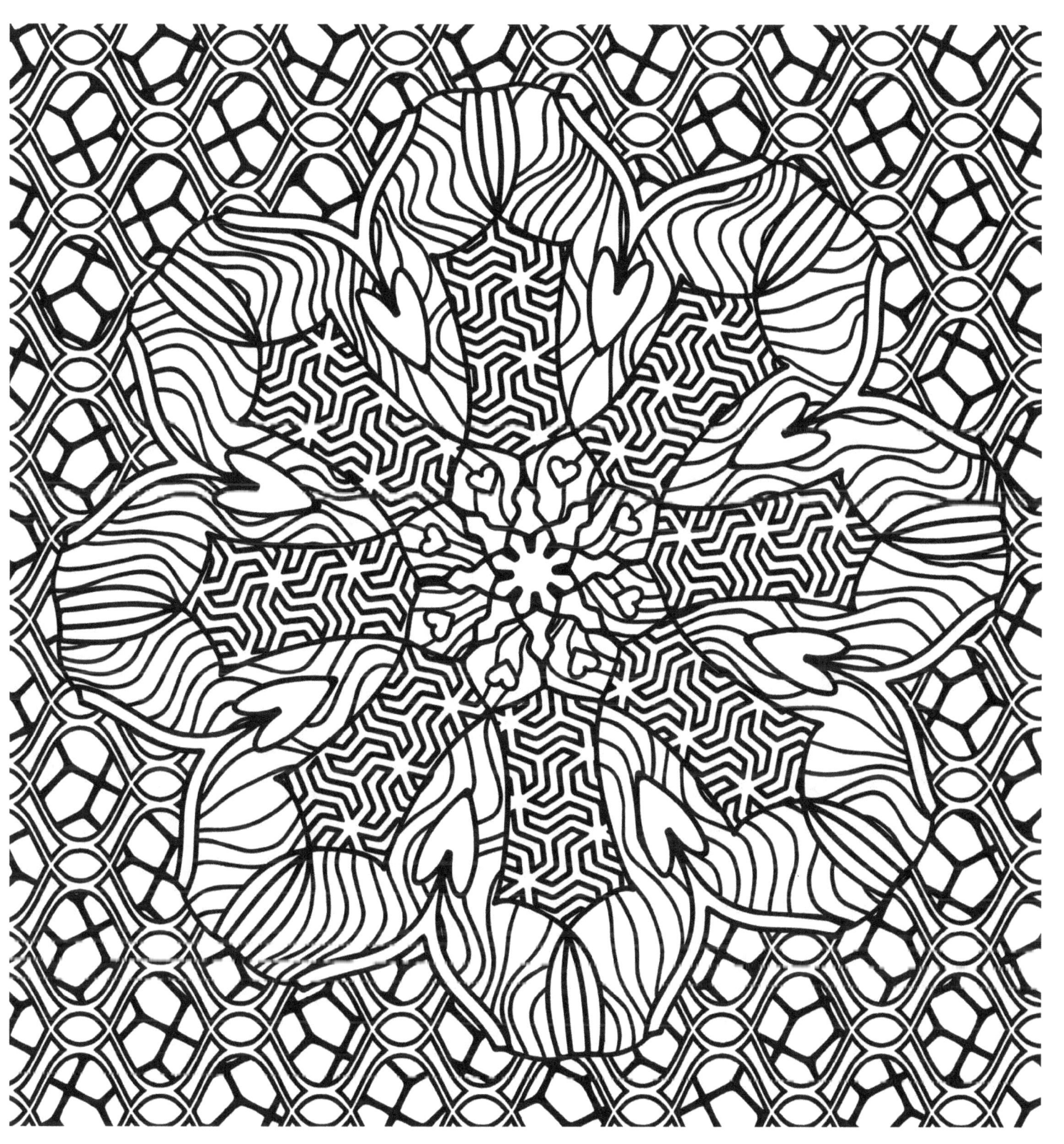

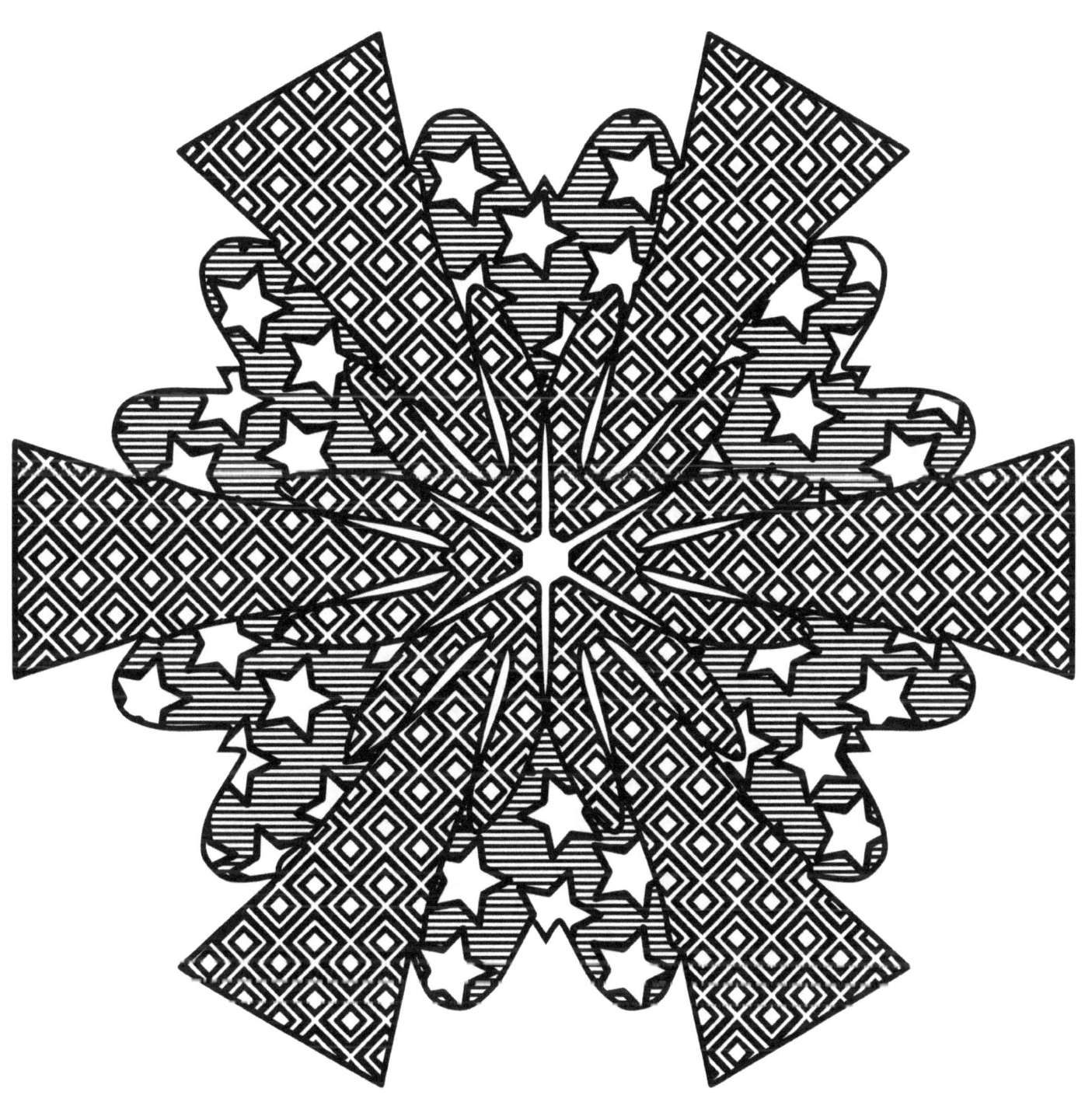

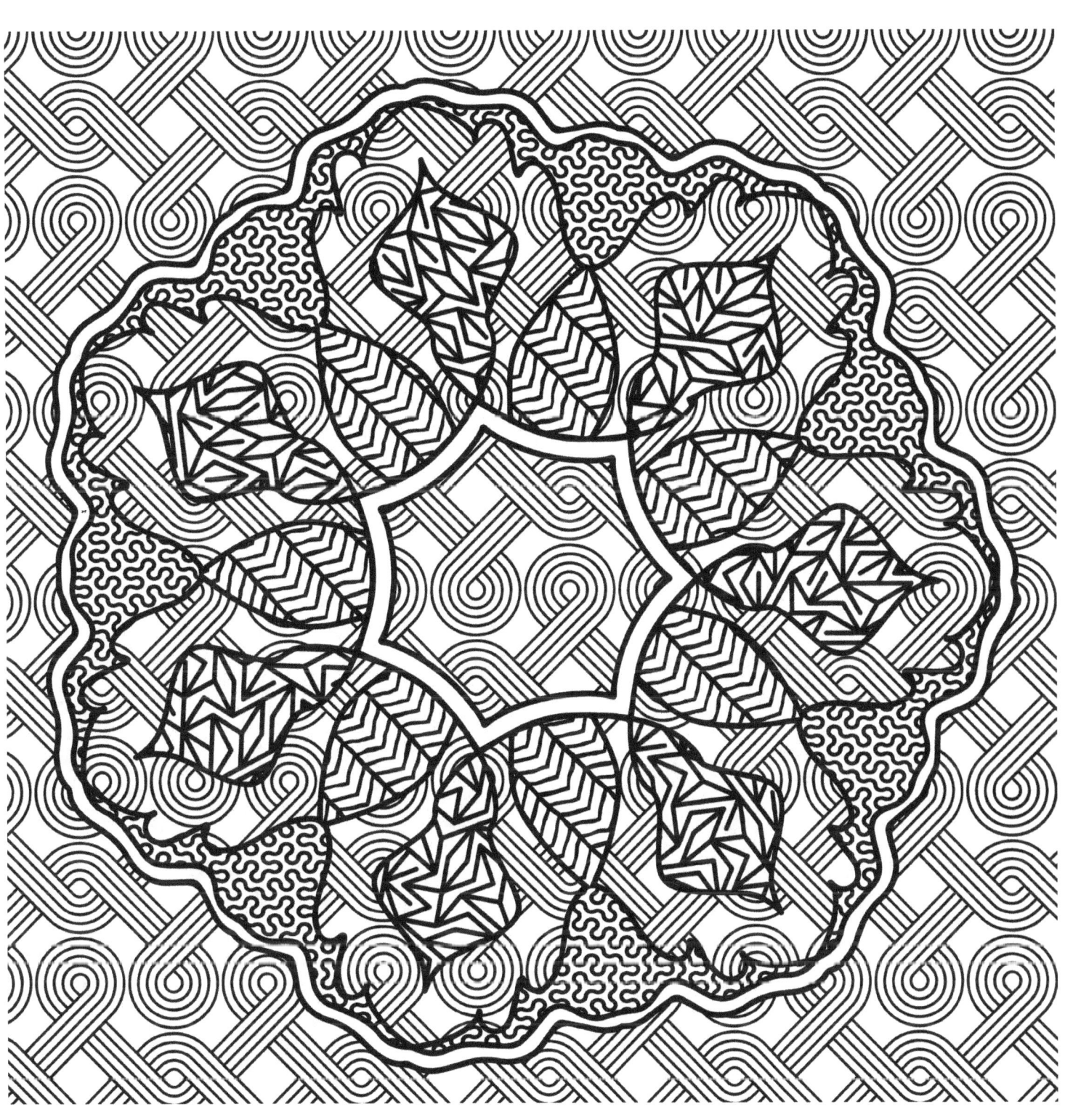

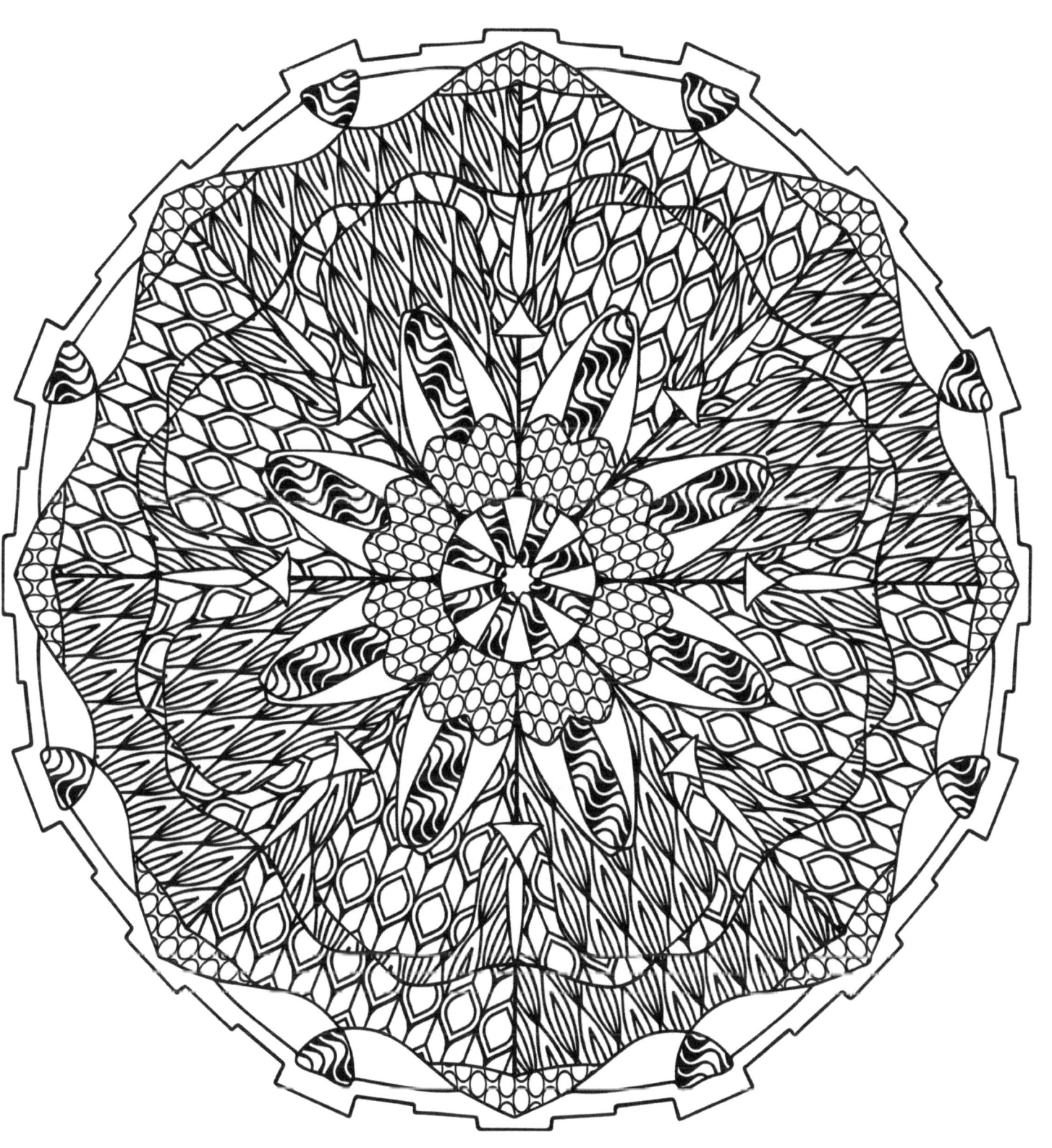

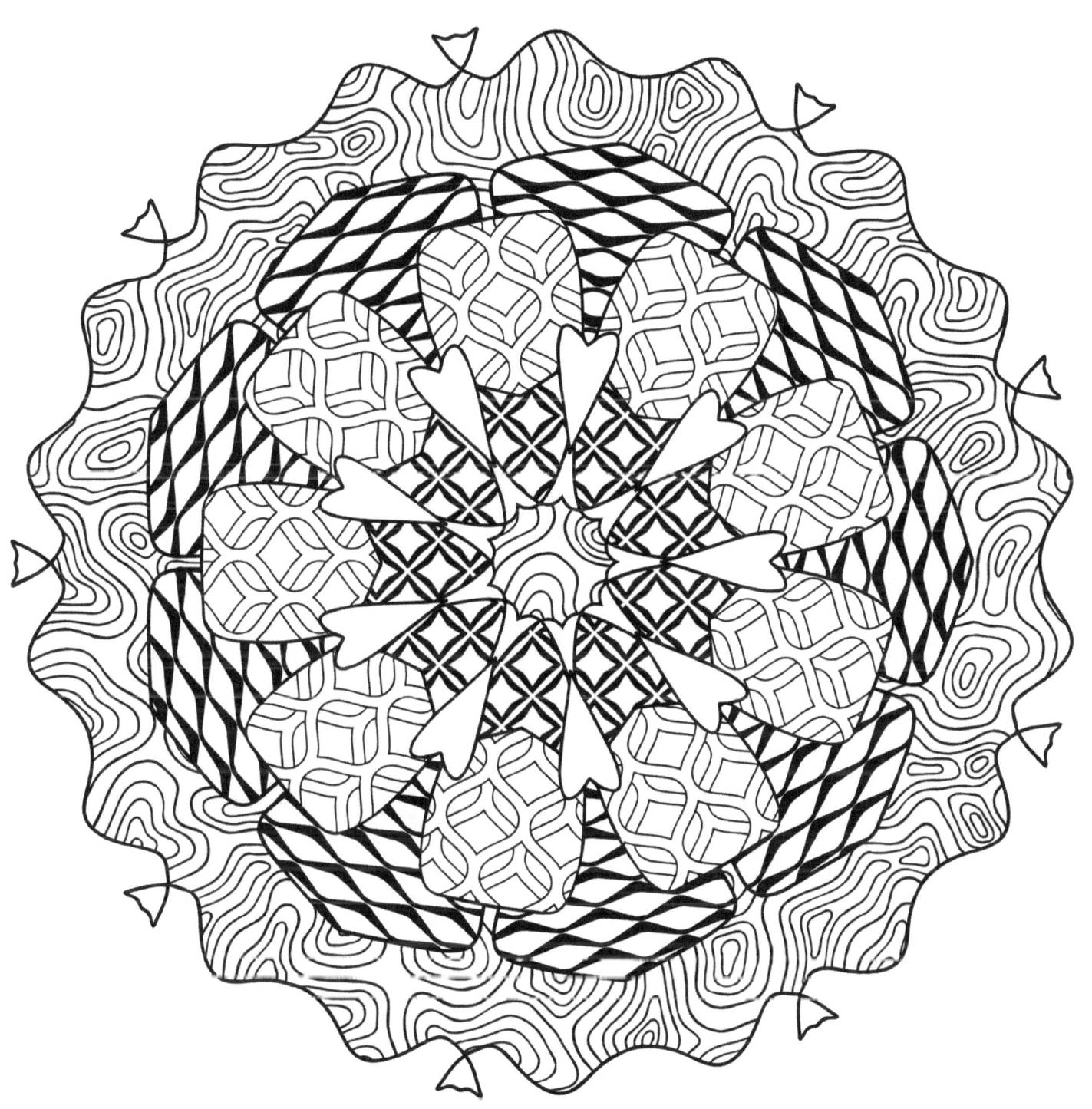

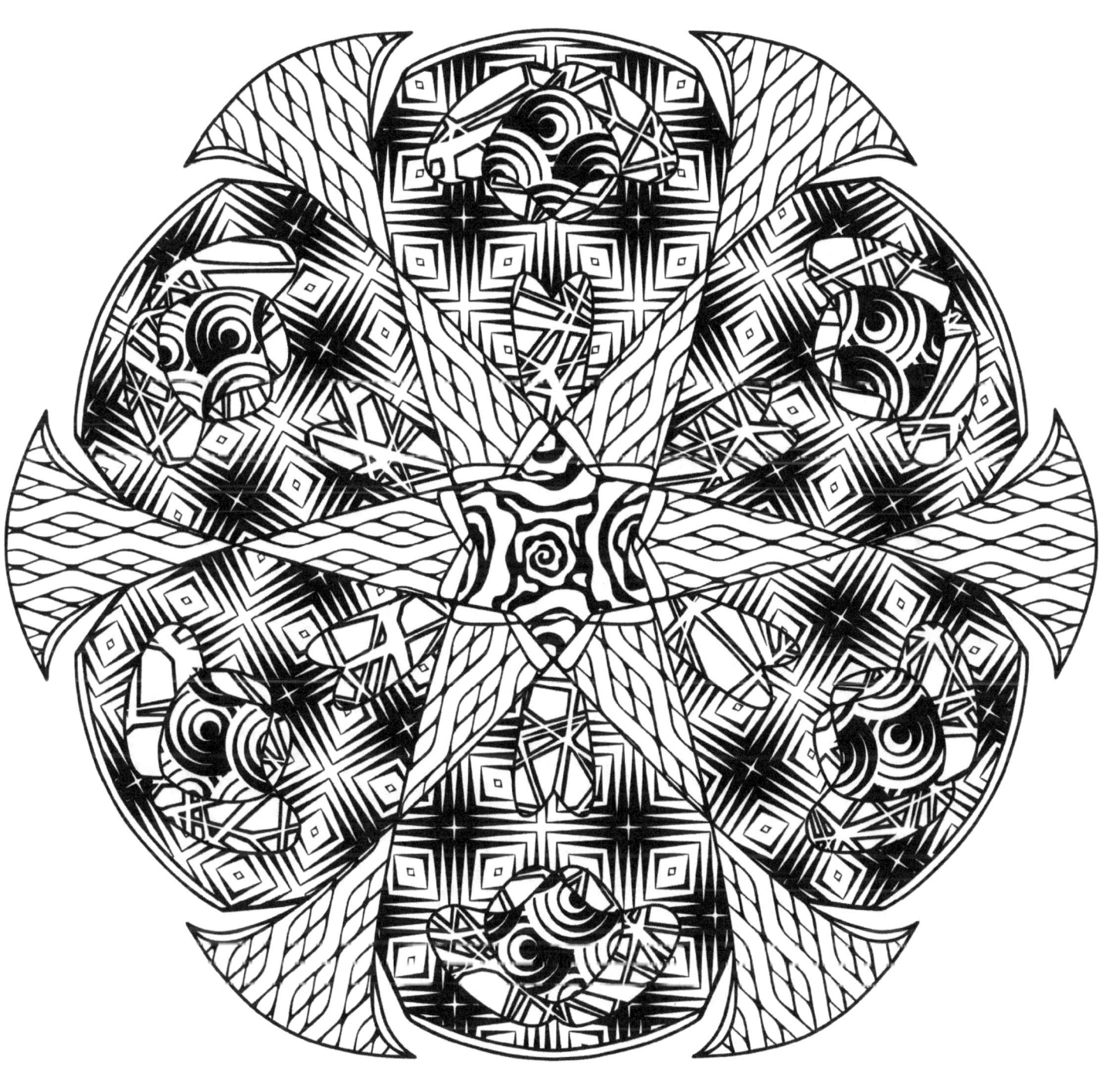

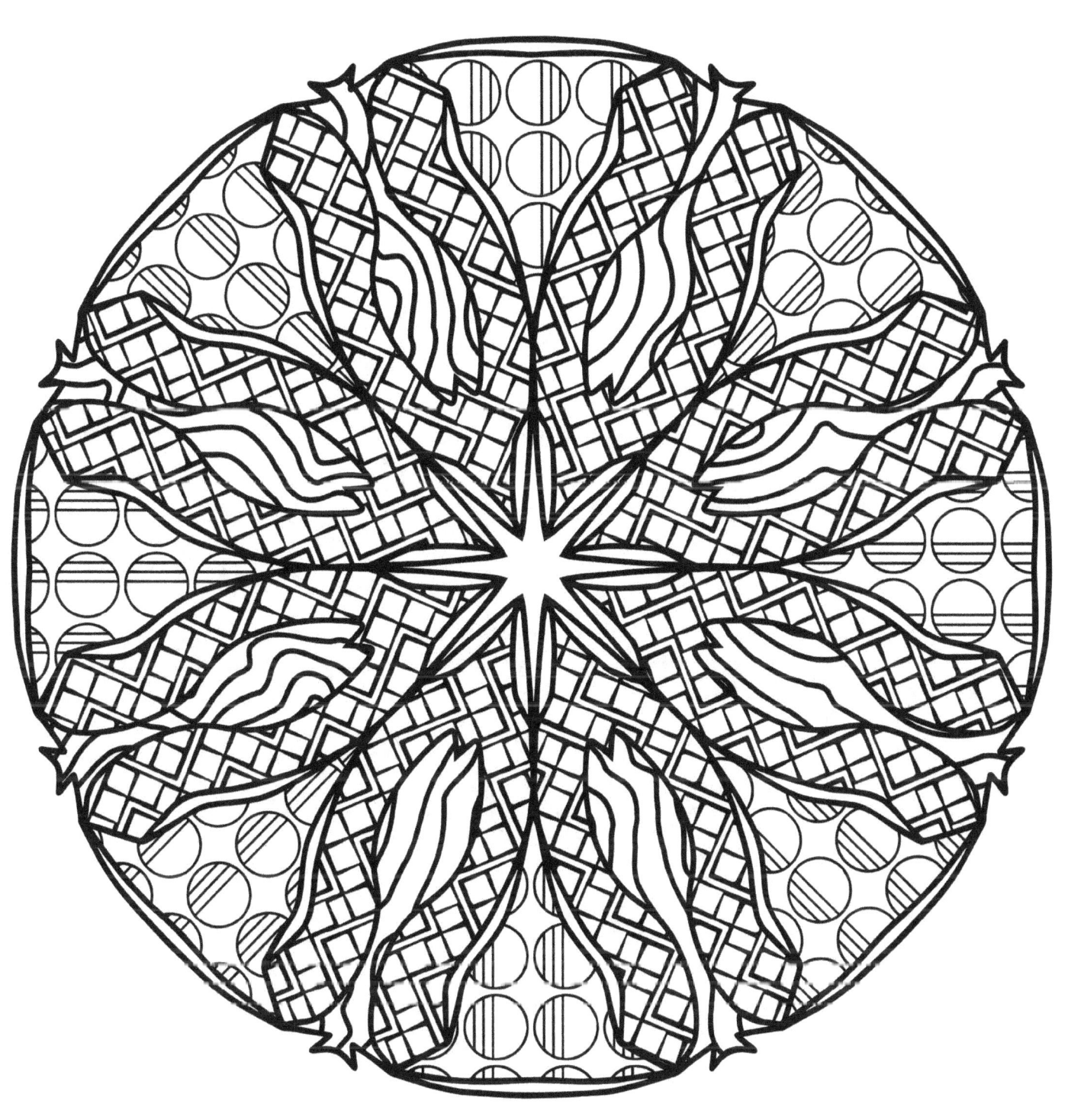

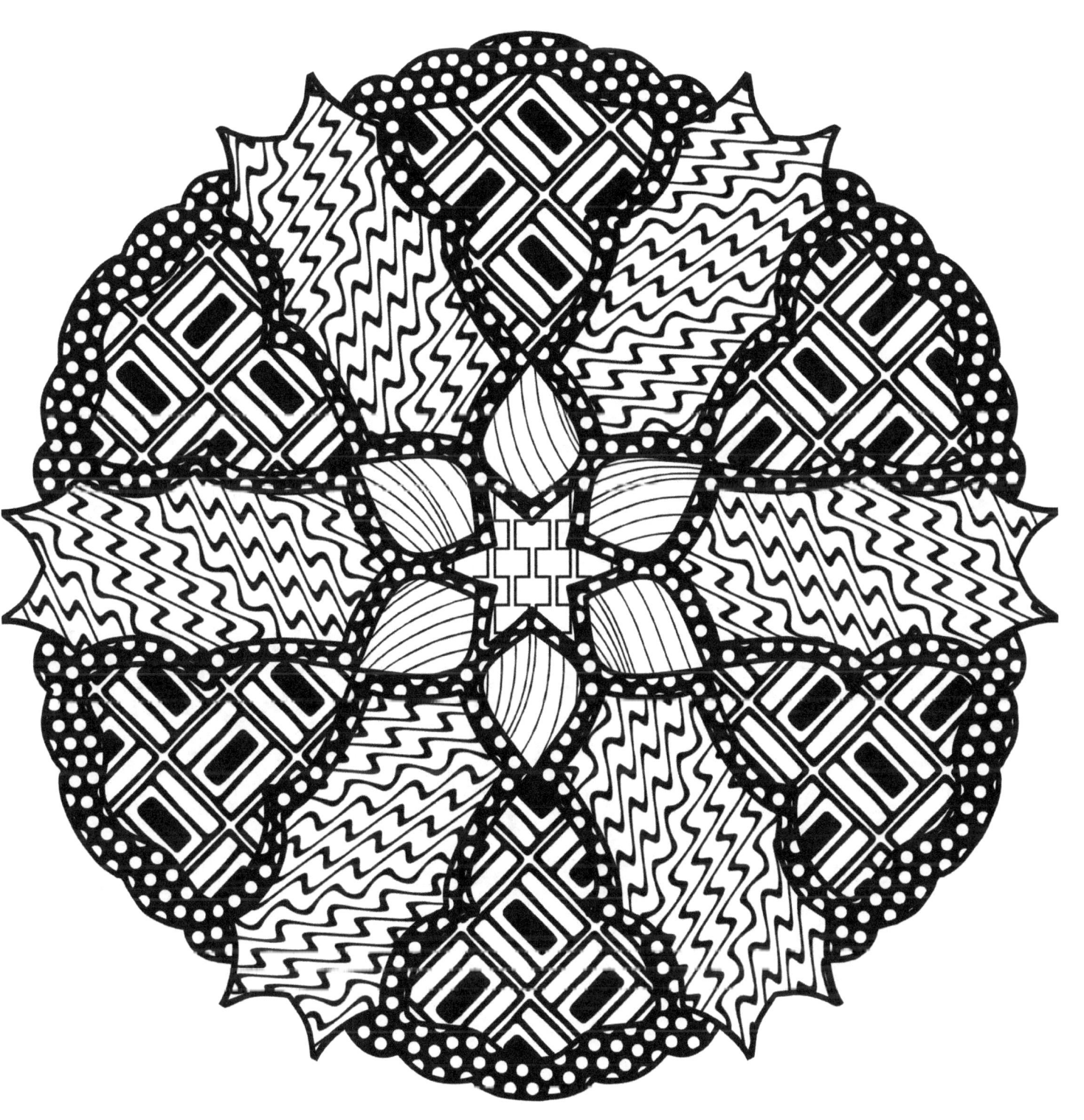

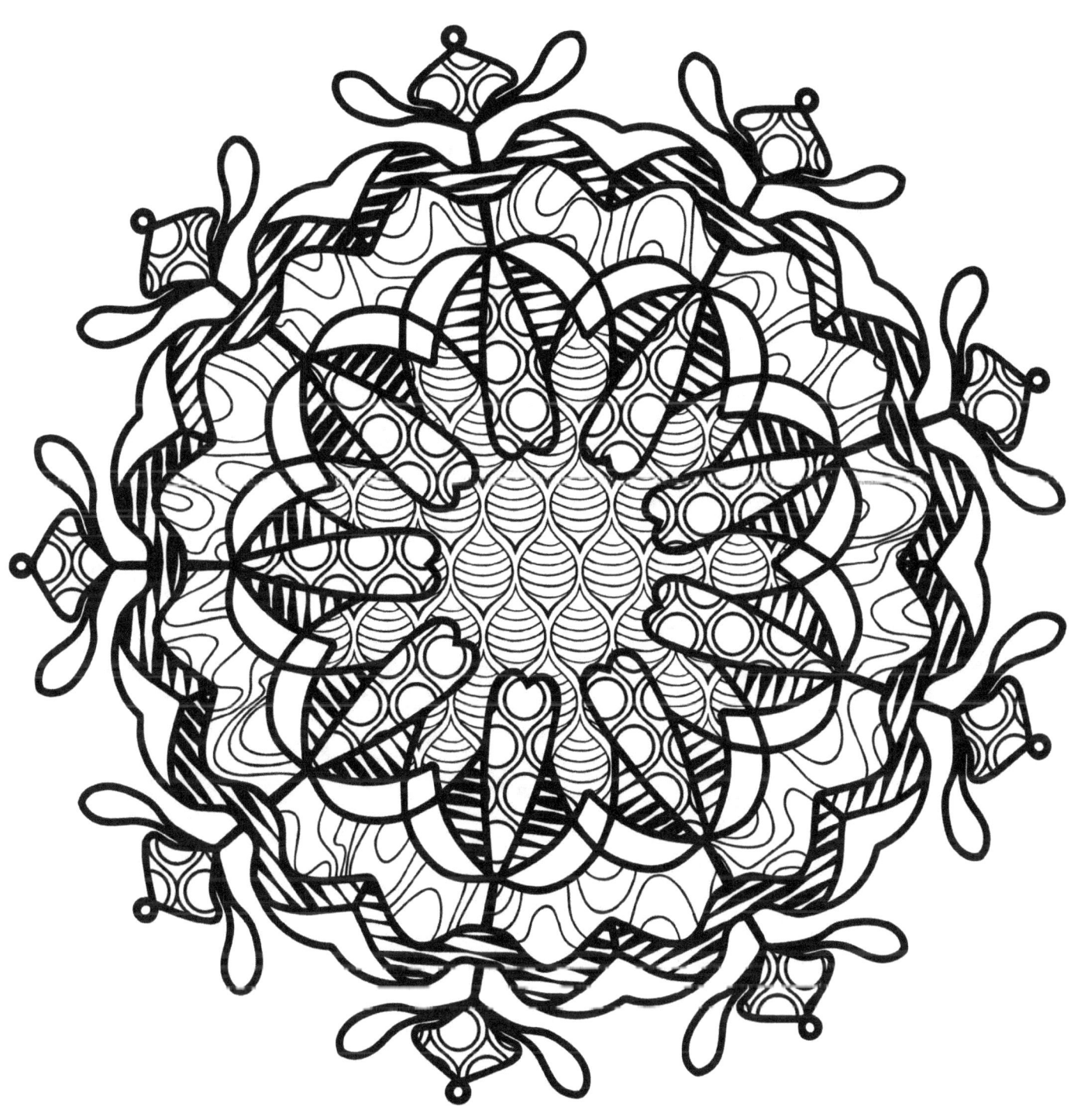

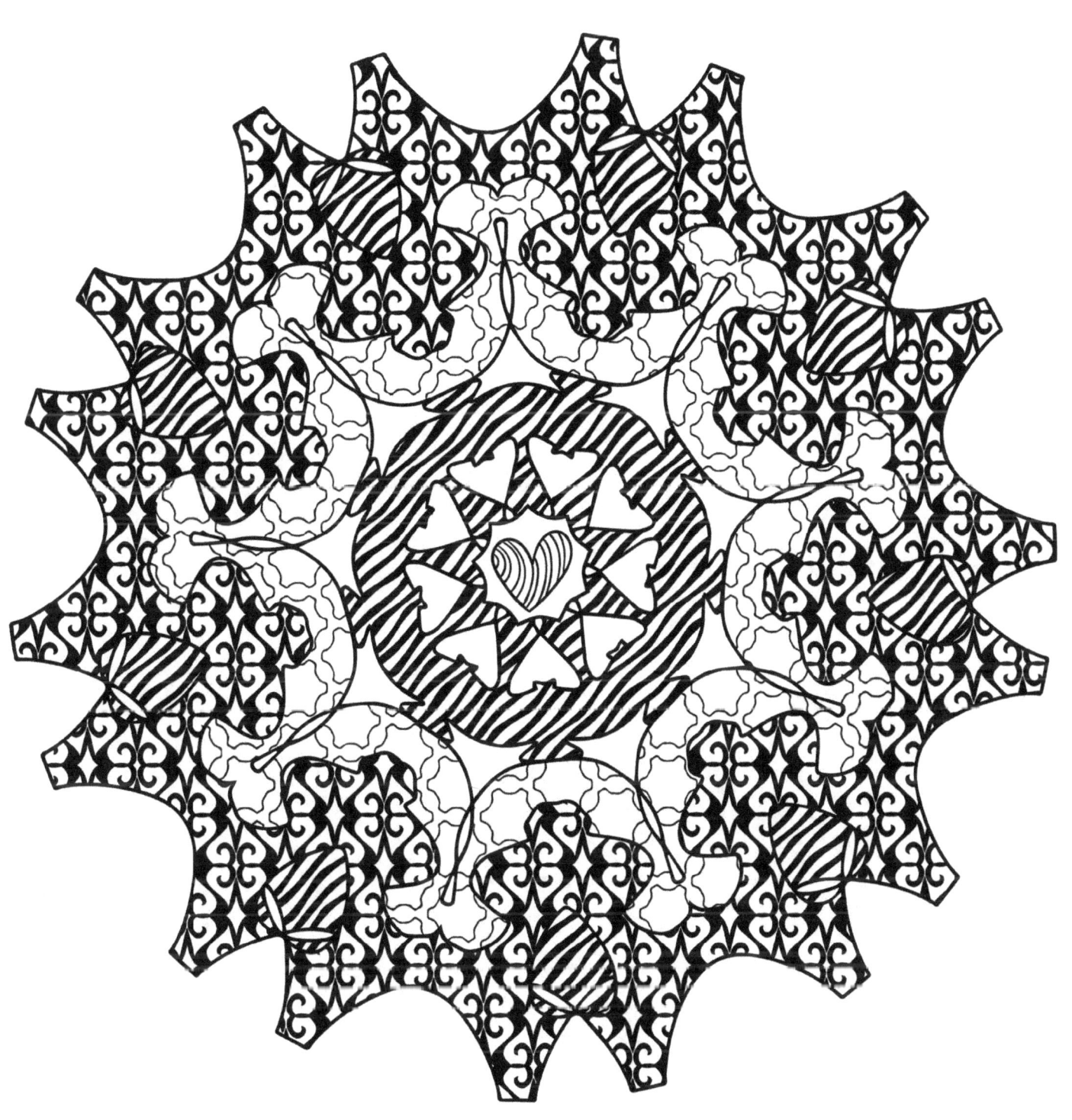

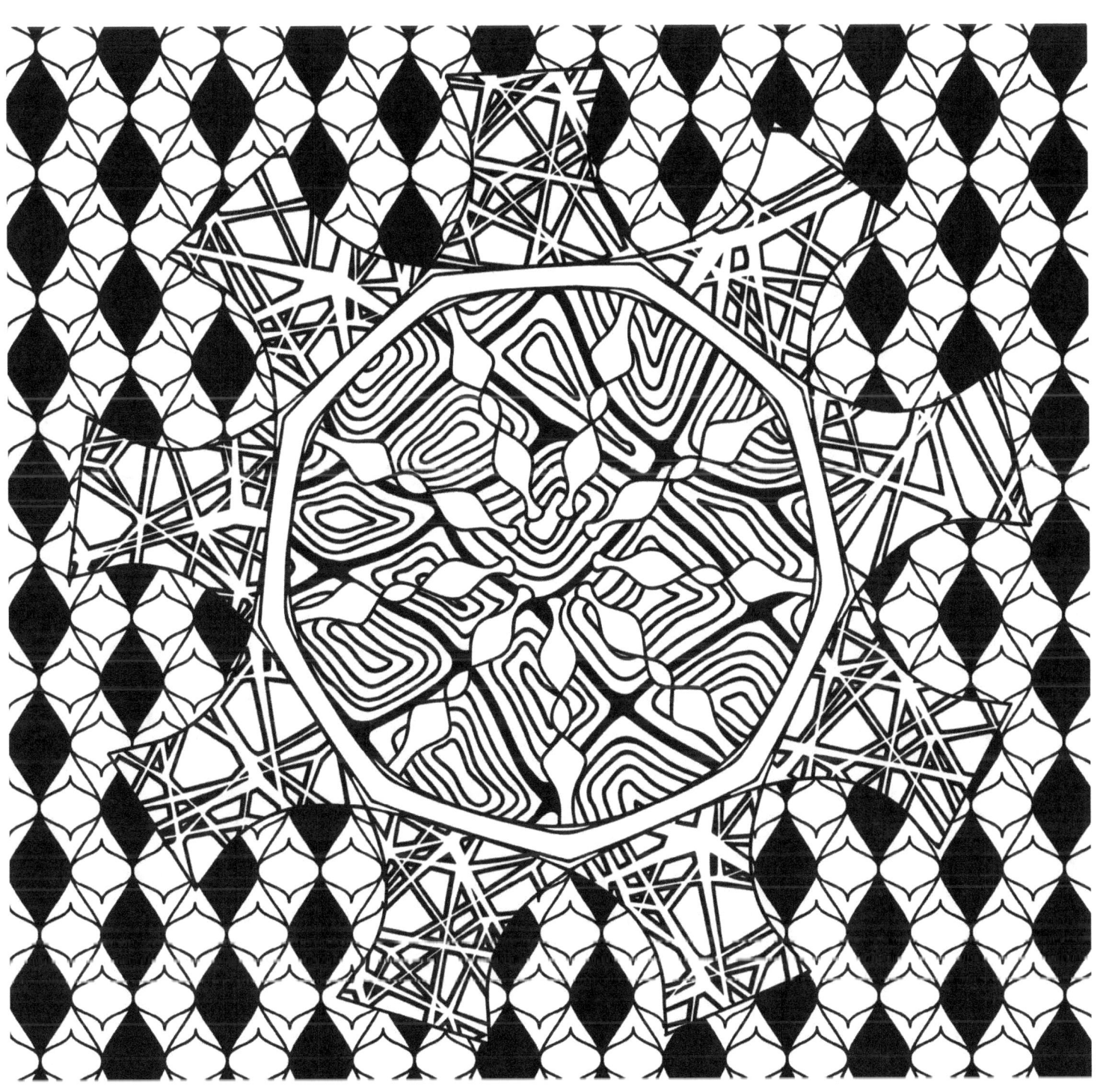

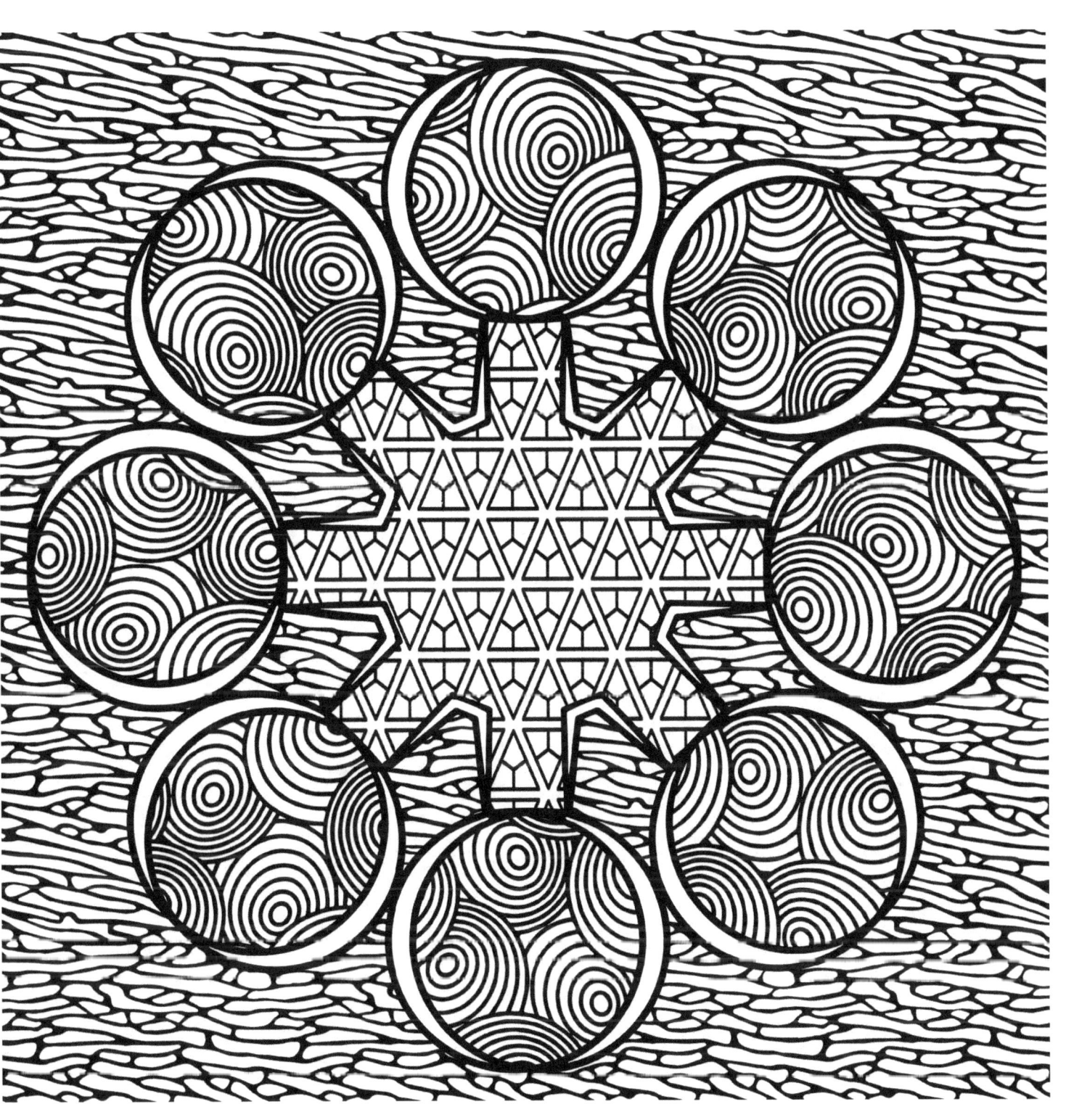

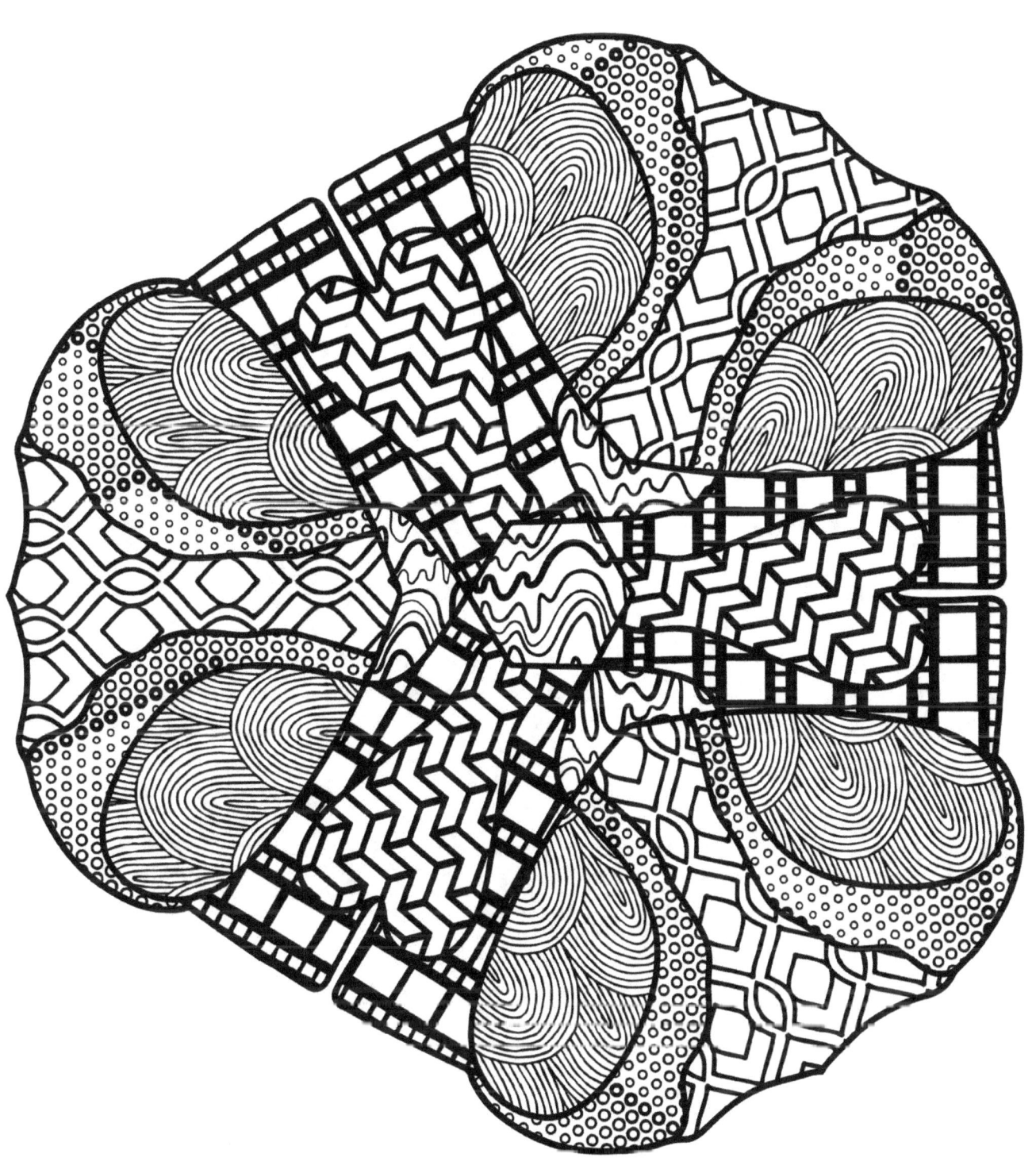

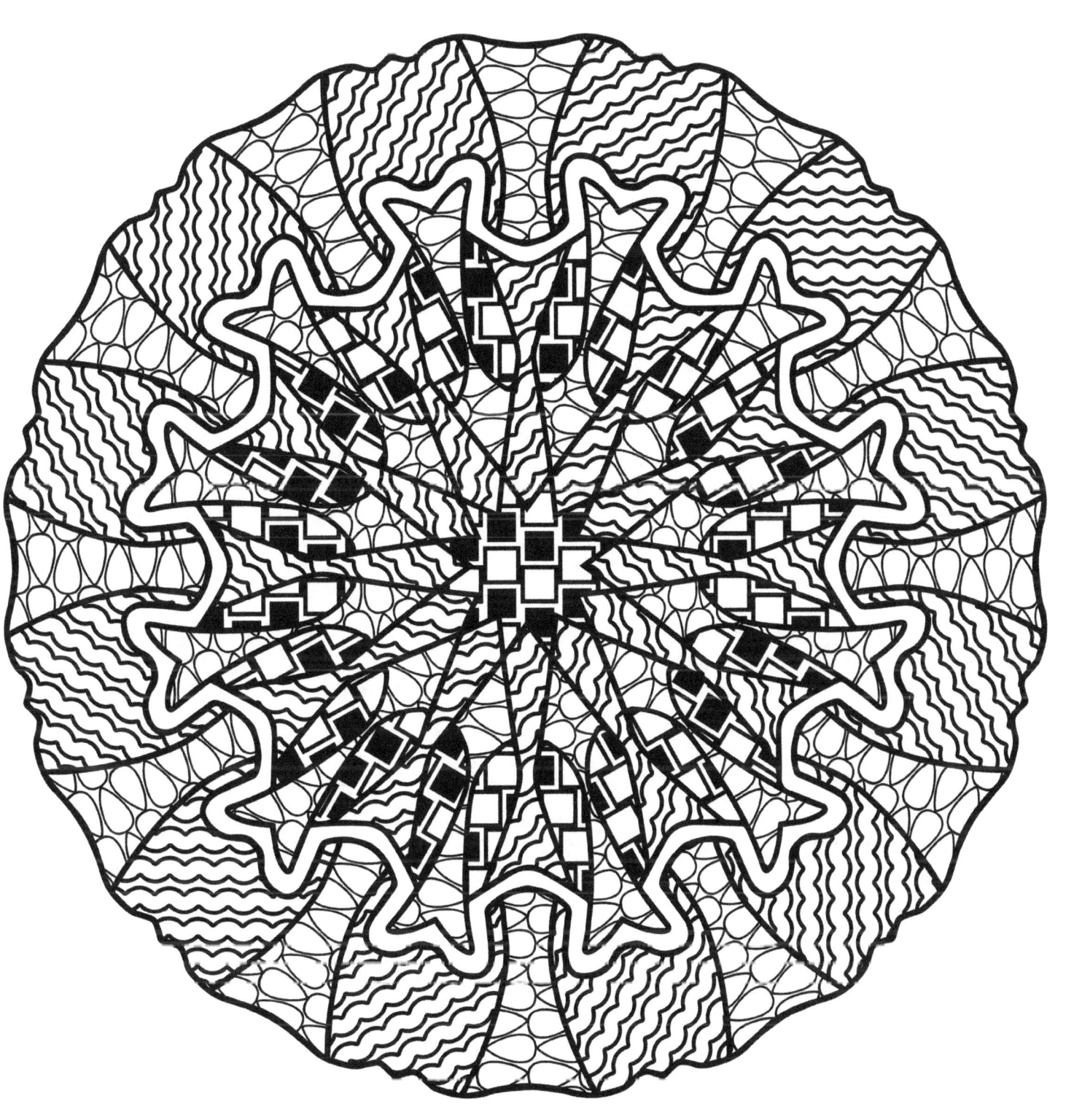

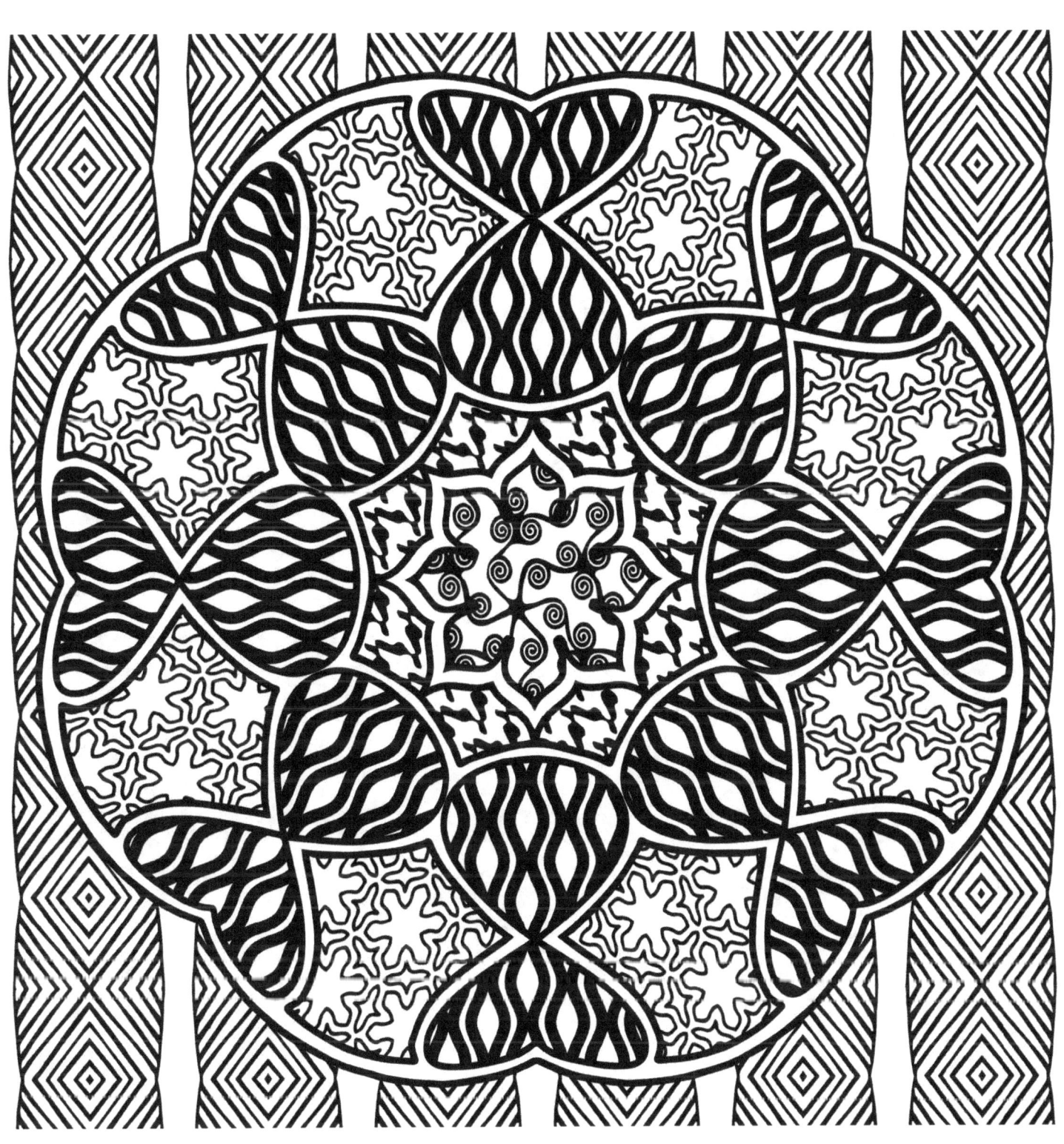

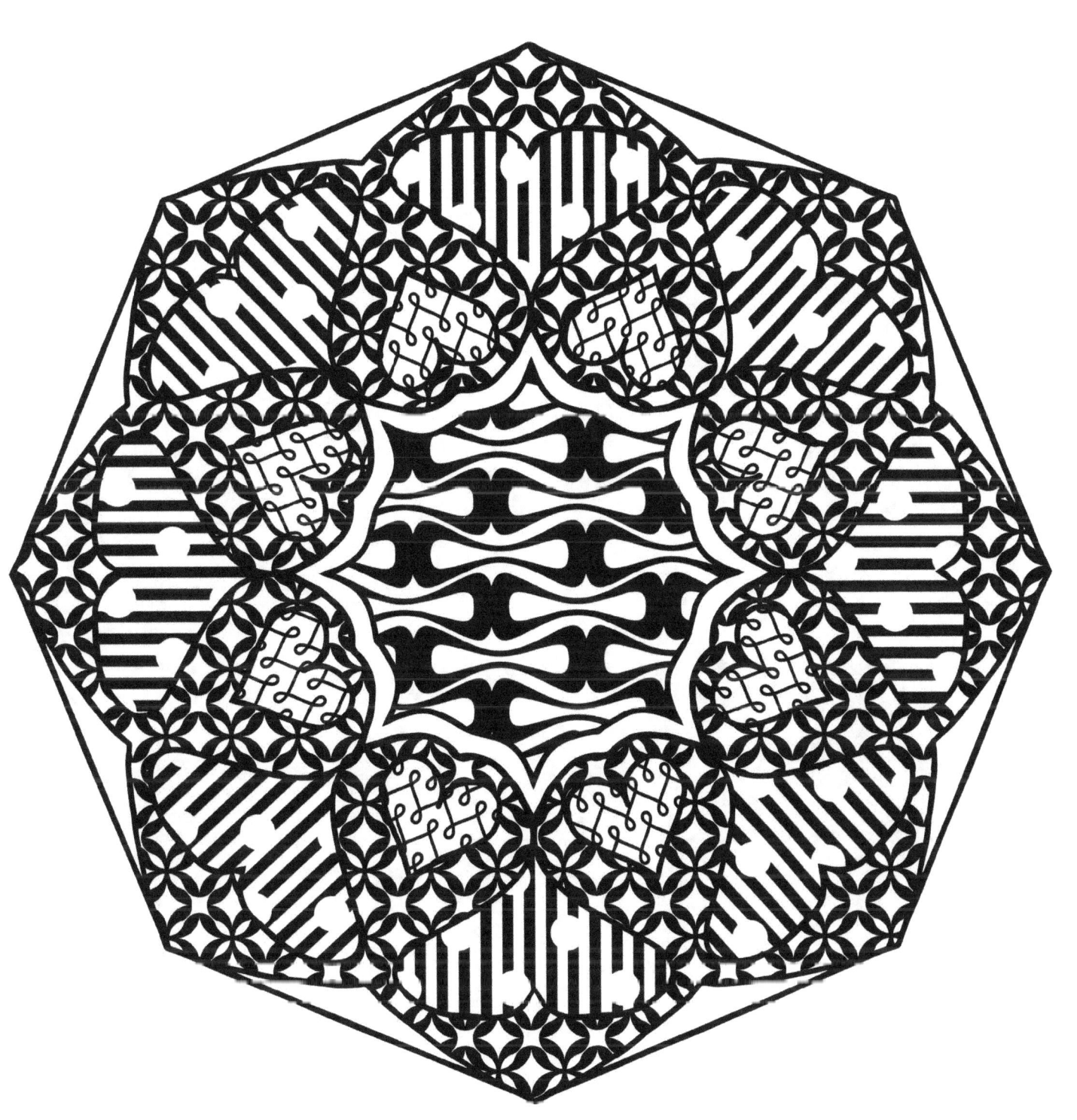

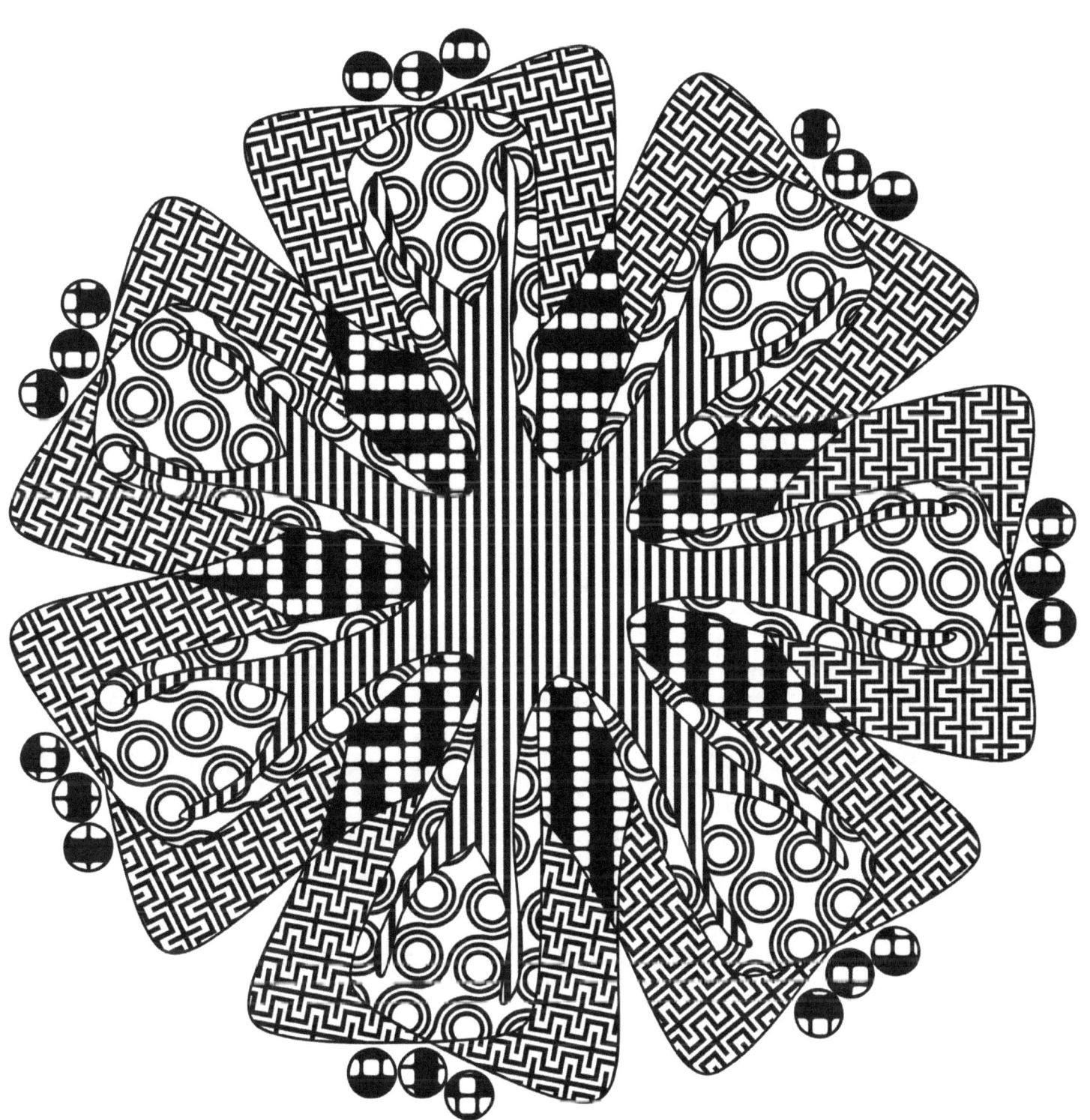

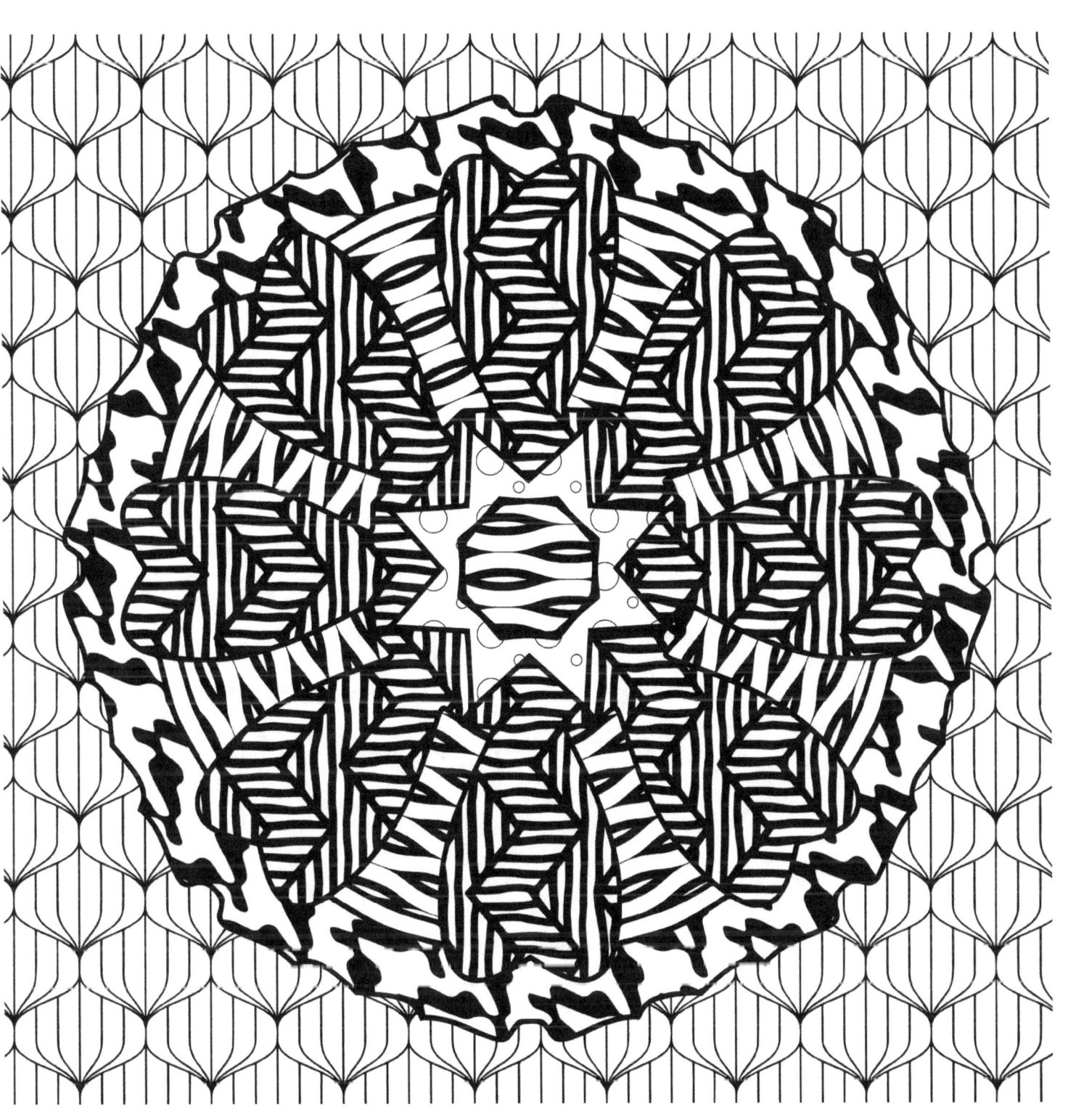

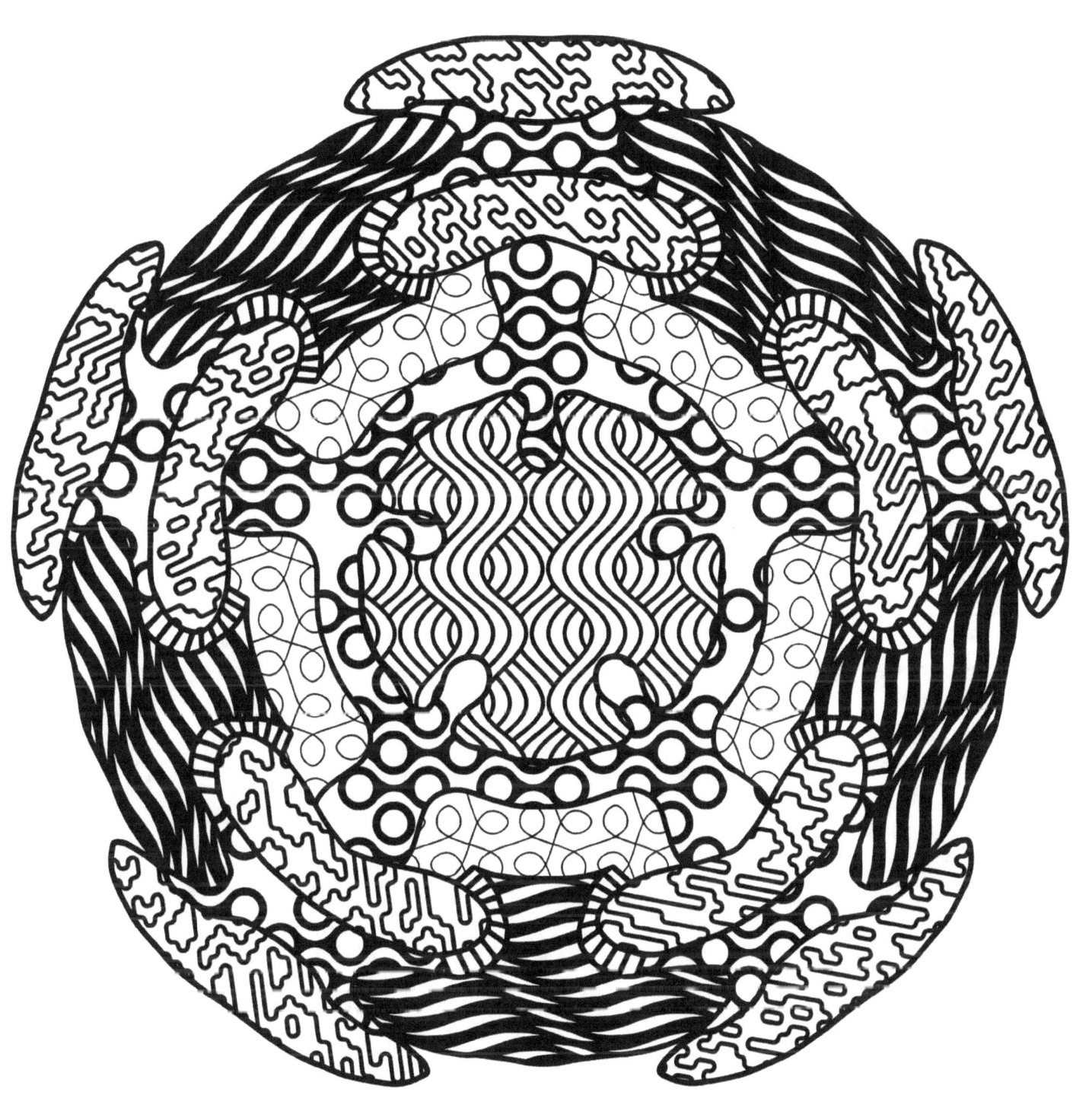

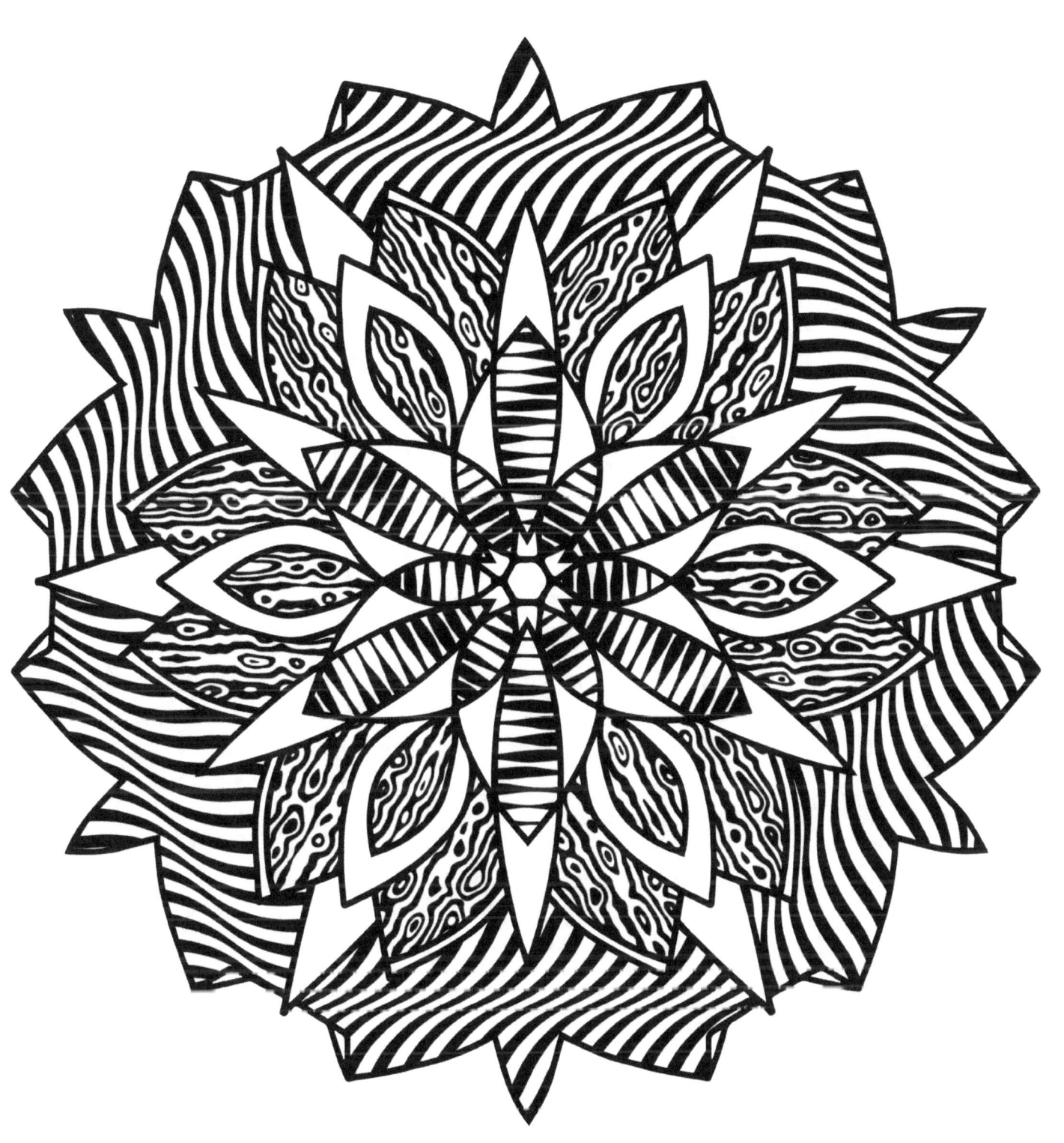

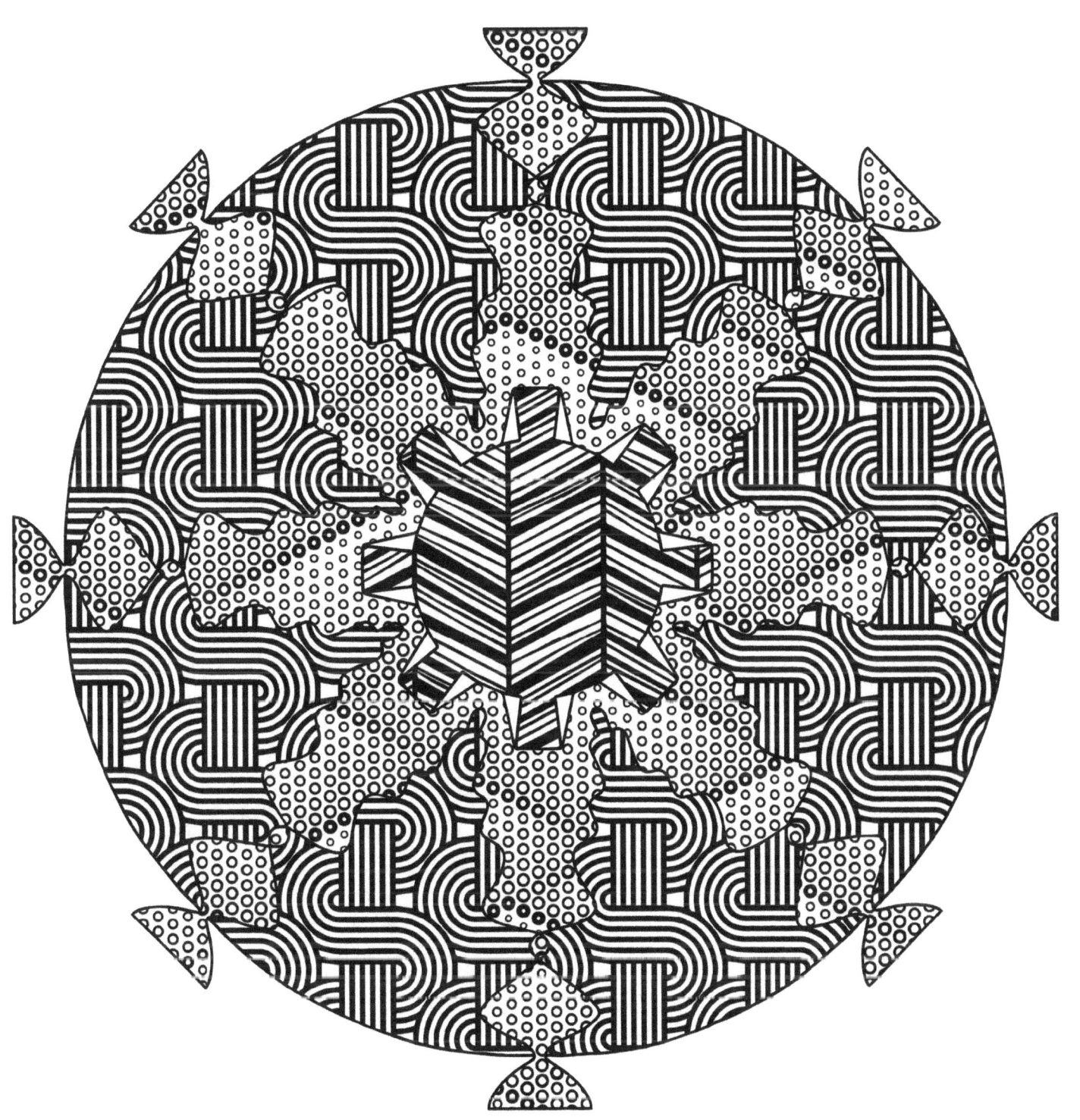